Meditations
on
Death
and
Life

Sterling W. Sill

International Standard Book Number
0-88290-212-1

Library of Congress Catalog Card Number
83-80406

Horizon Publishers Catalog and Order Number
1067

Third Printing, September 1987

& Distributors, Incorporated
50 South 500 West   P.O. Box 490
Bountiful, Utah 84010-0490

*Jacket and cover photography and design by
Richard Jamison.*

Contents

1

Foreword

The one business of our lives is to succeed. I am absolutely certain in my own mind that God did not go to all of the trouble of creating this beautiful earth with its many laws, resources, and opportunities without having something very special in mind for those who would be privileged to live upon it.

Certainly God did not endow us with these magnificent minds, these miraculous personalities, and these fantastic physical powers, and then expect us to waste our lives in failure. And yet I am sure of this—that the greatest waste there is in the world is not the devastation that goes with war, it is not the cost of crime, it is not the erosion of our soils, or the depletion of our raw materials, or the loss of our gold supply—the greatest waste there is in the world is that human beings, you and I, live so far below the level of our possibilities. Compared with what we might be, most of us are just partly alive.

At birth we came into a world which had a fantastic program for our improvement already laid out before us. Because of its extent, its science, its contrasts, and its complications, it is very difficult for us to comprehend the meaning of this program as we make this beginning in our lives. We are faced immediately with the idea of learning to read, to write, to make a living, to organize a family, and to communicate effectively with other people.

In this wonderful world there are very few of the most simple things that we actually understand when we are born. We don't understand light, or life, or how the grass grows, or how our minds operate. We don't really understand vision, or hearing, or speech, or love, or death, or birth.

We begin our lives with the idea that the greatest fact in the universe is God. He is the Creator of the universe. He is the designer of our lives. He is our Eternal Heavenly Father. He himself is immortal and has the power to

9

grant this blessing to His children. Without Him we would be nothing, but with Him we can become even as He is. He pronounced the future possibilities of a group of His children by saying to them, ". . . Ye are gods; and all of you are children of the most High" (Psalms 82:6).

The gospel might be compared with something similar to a book of instructions which we get when we purchase a new television set, or an automobile, or a can opener, to tell us how to proceed. But the gospel is much more than that. It gives us detailed instructions for an eternal life of the greatest success and happiness, if we will only follow the all-wise directions we have been given.

It is impossible for us to learn all the details for ourselves that God understood as He designed our world, our lives, and our program. How ridiculous is the logic of the skeptic who said that he would not believe anything that he was unable to understand and explain. Certainly the list of beliefs and accomplishments of such a one would be very short since even the greatest medical men cannot make one single red corpuscle, nor can the greatest scientists construct one kernel of wheat that will grow.

There are a great many things we do not need to understand if we have enough faith to say we believe in God. The God story tells us that He is our Eternal Heavenly Father, who created us in His image and endowed us with a full set of His attributes and potentialities. He made all the preparations necessary for our eternal exaltation and happiness if we will only follow His all-wise directions.

The second most important fact in the universe is that we are the children of God, created in His image, that God loves us and is interested in our welfare, and that He has given us life. If we are obedient, He will give us the same kind of life and happiness and success that He has.

This is an idea of such grandeur that when Jesus discussed it with the Pharisees of His own day, and told them that He was the Son of God, they accused Him of blasphemy and went about trying to kill Him. And yet our program of exaltation is so marvelous that some people still have almost as much trouble in accepting it as did the unbelieving Pharisees.

Also, our success in life is frequently interrupted because, like the skeptic, we have so many doubts that we tend to lose our way. We may have the finest television set, but if we do not follow the instructions telling us how to connect it with electricity and work the controls properly, it will not produce as promised in the book of instructions. And when we pervert our lives with sin, we are like the scientist who does not follow the laws of his science and therefore, like him, we do not reach the desired end.

The gospel tells us about the plan of life and salvation. It pictures three great areas of life. The scriptures tell us clearly about an ante-mortal estate where we prepared for this life, which is somewhat like a finishing school where we get ready for eternity. Our birth into this life signals the end of our ante-mortal existence, and our death in this life signals the beginning of eternity.

The dates marking the end of our ante-mortal existence and this existence are among the most important ones in our lives. But if we do not understand them, or if we do not have faith in the word of the Lord, we may be thrown off our projected course.

An interesting commentary is that, next to God, we ordinarily know less about our individual selves than anything else. If you ask a man about science, or invention, or history, or politics, he will answer you. But if you ask him to write out an analysis of himself which will tell about his mind and soul qualities, you may not get a very good answer. Or if you ask him where he came from, what his purpose in life is, or where he is going beyond this life, he may stand silent and uncomprehending before you.

Each of us should keep in mind that man is a duality. The scripture says, "(In the beginning God) created the heaven and the earth and all things that in them are" (3 Nephi 9:15). He gave a little more detail of these two creations when He said,

". . . I, the Lord God, made the heaven and the earth;

"And every plant of the field before it was in the earth, and every herb of the field before it grew. For I, the Lord God, created all . . . the children of men; and not yet a man to till the ground; for in heaven created I them; and there was not yet flesh upon the earth, neither in the water, neither in the air." (Moses 3:4-5.)

After our ante-mortal existence, we live during mortality with the spirit and the body subject to separation, since death is one of the inescapable necessities for the exaltation of ourselves or our souls. And while no one in this life has seen his own spirit, yet each of us is aware that we have one.

Anyone who has ever stood at the bier of a loved one has been made conscious of the fact that the real essence of the person he loved has departed; that he is looking upon the shell that merely housed the spirit. Sometimes we fail to understand that the spirit exists when we cannot see it, and yet we know that the really important part of a person departs from the body at the time of death. Some people also have problems in believing in the actuality of the resurrection.

Many quotations will be given in the following pages from the scriptures and from the logic of what other great minds have believed. It is hoped that what follows will be a means of offering comfort and consolation at the time of bereavement, or at times when we may want to think about this event of death which shall some day come to us . . . as, indeed, it surely will.

2

Life's Greatest Adventure

In 1904, the Scottish playwright, Sir James M. Barrie, published his famous story, "Peter Pan." The story was a big hit from the very beginning and later was made into a full-length animated cartoon.

As a young boy, Peter Pan overheard his parents discussing what they wanted their son to do when he grew up. Because Peter didn't want to do any of the things he heard his parents talking about, he decided that instead of growing up he would run away from home and live with the fairies. Peter Pan wanted to spend the rest of his life in that enchanting world of make-believe called "Never-Never Land," where he did not have to do any of the work of adults but could spend his entire time enjoying himself in the adolescent pleasures of having fun.

On one occasion Peter was overtaken by a serious adversity and felt sure that he was going to drown. In his great stress he said to himself, "Death will be an awfully big adventure." And so it will be for all of us. But as death is a big adventure, so also is life a big adventure. Living effectively is also the best way to have fun. Happiness is the purpose of life itself. The prophet Lehi said to his own son, Jacob, "Man is that he might have joy" (2 Nephi 2:25).

Abraham Lincoln once said, "A man is about as happy as he makes up his mind to be." And he is also about as wise and as successful and as godly as he makes up his mind to be. We all need a lot of adventure and genuine fun and happiness, which is largely a spiritual process.

Edwin Dyer once said,

> My mind to me a kingdom is;
> Such present joys therein I find,
> That it excels all other bliss
> That earth affords or grows by kind;

Man does not live by bread alone. A great playwrite wrote a play in which he has his leading character, Rudolph, say:

"If you'll go stop three tradesmen on the street and ask the three what it is they live by, they will reply at once, 'Bread, Meat, and Drink;' and they will be certain of it. Victuals and drink, like the rhyme in Mother Goose, make up their diet. Nothing will be said of faith in things unseen or of following the gleam. Just bread and meat and a can of wine to wash it down. But if you know them well; if you know them better than they do, each one burns candles at some altar of his mind in secret—secret often from himself. Each is a priest to some dim mystery by which he lives. Strip him of that, and bread and meat and wine won't nourish him. Without this hidden faith, he dies and goes to dust." And someone has pointed out that we can live on less if we have more to live for.

And God has ordained for us the great adventure of life, beginning with birth and ending with death and leading to His greatest gift of eternal life in His presence, which certainly gives us the most important objective to live for. Solomon said, "There is a time to be born and a time to die." And there are a great many other wonderful experiences that may come in between.

Sometime ago, I heard the President of the Church say to the General Authorities that he thought every Church member, especially the General Authorities, should write their biography and thereafter keep a biographical account of their lives. Because I like to do what the President of the Church suggests, I got started the next morning to carry out his instructions.

As best I could, I went back in memory over my life and tried to make some appraisals of those places where I thought I had done well and where I thought improvements could be made. I discovered a startling point of view: that the greatest accomplishment of my life, the fact that I appreciated more than any other thing, was that I was successful in getting myself born. I cannot describe how pleased I was about my particular good fortune that I was alive and had an inheritance upon this earth.

At a little later date, I was talking to a group of young people and I congratulated them on being born in this great age of wonders and enlightenment that Apostle Paul referred to as "the dispensation of the fullness of times." After the meeting, a young man came up and disclaimed any credit. He said he had nothing to do with bringing about his own birth. But he was wrong. He had everything to do with it.

Someone has tried to help us understand life by comparing it to a three-act play. We had a long ante-mortal experience which might be called the first act. Then we have a little, short mortality which might be referred to as the second act. Then we have the possibility of a long, everlasting immortality which we could refer to as the third act.

Someone has said that if we went into the theater after the first act had been finished and left before the third act began, we may not understand the play. Life just does not make sense, sometimes, when we look at it from too limited a perspective.

The early American philosopher, Henry Thoreau, once said that we should thank God every morning when we get up for the privilege of having been born. Then he went on to speculate on the rather unique supposition of what it might have been like if we had never been born, and he mentioned a number of those exciting and uplifting experiences that would have been missed as a consequence.

What Mr. Thoreau may not have known was that one-third of all the children of God followed the rebellion of Lucifer in their ante-mortal estate, and were denied the privilege forever of a mortal probation and all of the wonderful experiences that are included for us because we earned the right to enjoy them. We earned this right because we followed God during our first estate in opposing the rebellion of Lucifer.

There is a great scripture in Matthew having to do with the second act in the life of Jesus, the Son of God the Father, who was appointed to redeem us from death. Matthew said:

"Now when Jesus was born in Bethlehem of Judea in the days of Herod the king, behold, there came wise men from the east of Jerusalem,

"Saying, Where is he that is born King of the Jews? for we have seen his star in the east, and are come to worship him." (Matt. 2:1-2.)

And that is what wise men and women have been doing ever since that time.

The greatest tragedy of our world of 2,000 years ago was that so many people failed to find the King during their second estate. They saw Him walk down the street, they heard Him preach in the temple, they knew of His miracles, they ate of His loaves and fishes, but they refused to carry His cross, or accept Him as their Savior.

We live 2,000 years later and have had many additional experiences with the judgment of time shining upon the life of Christ. The most exciting thought that I am capable of thinking is that we have been granted this mortal probation when the gospel of Jesus Christ has been restored to the earth in its fullness, and we are able to follow that program which will lead us to finding the King and enjoying eternal life in His presence.

President Joseph Fielding Smith frequently said the most important part of our eternal lives is the few years of mortality we experience on this earth. We passed all the requirements of our first estate with flying colors. We have seen God; He is our Eternal Heavenly Father. We lived with Him during our pre-existence. Now all that stands between us and an everlasting eternal life in His presence is what we do during these few years here in mortality.

Edgar A. Guest once wrote an exciting adventure poem which would make Peter Pan's greatest ambition for fun seem very unexciting. It might have been a conversation carried on between you and God as you prepared to make your transition into this life. The idea of this poem was suggested by the discussion on free agency in the Council in Heaven. Mr. Guest entitled his poem, "Uninstructed."

> I'm going to send you down to earth
>   Said God to me one day.
> I'm giving you what men call birth,
>   Tonight you'll start away.
> I want you there to live with men
>   Until I call you back again.
>
> I trembled as I heard him speak,
>   Yet I knew that I must go.
> I felt his hand upon my cheek
>   And wished that I might know
> What on the earth would be my task
>   And timidly I dared to ask.
>
> Tell me before I start away
>   What thou wouldst have me do.
> What message thou wouldst have me say.
>   When will my work be through?
> That I may serve thee on the earth
>   Tell me the purpose of my birth.
>
> God smiled at me and softly said,
>   Oh, you shall find your task.
> I want you free life's paths to tread
>   So do not stay to ask.
> Remember that if your best you do
>   That I shall ask no more of you.

Then Mr. Guest said:

> How often as my work I do
>   So common-place and grim
> I sit and sigh and wish I knew
>   If I were pleasing him,
> I wonder if with every test
>   I've really tried to do my best.

Many of us have felt this same way. We would like to have a mid-term report card with a percentage score upon it to let us know whether or not we are pleasing God. But there are no mid-term report cards in life. We must wait until the evidence is all in and the decisions have been made and the judgments handed down. Then we will find out for the first time how we fared during our second estate.

There are some people who claim to have difficulty in believing in eternal life. It has never seemed to me that it should be very difficult for anyone to believe in eternal life who can believe in his own birth. That is, if you can believe in this—that two microscopic bits of protoplasm can come together to create a life cell and then by a process of self-division can create other cells completely unlike the original to make this great masterpiece of flesh and blood, brain and personality, and spirit of godliness that we refer to as a human being—it ought not be difficult to believe that this great creation of God, once established, could continue to live throughout eternity.

Edwin Markham put this idea in verse when he wrote his poem referring to life itself as, "The Unbelievable."

> Impossible, you say, that man survives
> The grave—that there are other lives
> More strange, O friend, that we should ever rise
> Out of the dark to walk below these skies.
> (But) Once having risen into life and light,
> We need not wonder at our deathless flight.
>
> Life is the unbelievable; but now
> That this Incredible has taught us how,
> We can believe the all-imagining Power
> That breathed the Cosmos forth as a golden flower,
> Had potence in his breath
> To plan us new surprises beyond death—
> New spaces and new goals
> For the adventure of ascending souls.
>
> Be brave, O heart, be brave:
> It is not strange that man survives the grave:
> 'Twould be a stranger thing were he destroyed
> Than that he ever vaulted from the void.

3

The Beginning and the End of Life

Usually when we write the story of anyone's life, we begin at his birth and end at his death. But this is not completely accurate, as one's birth is the end of his pre-existence and the beginning of his mortality, whereas his death is but the end of his mortality and his birth into eternal life.

Among the two most important events in the life of the Savior were His birth and death. It was for the people of our earth a great blessing when Christ was born here on this earth. The celebration of His birth takes a prominent place in our lives. However, it is in connection with His death that He made some of His greatest contributions, including the atonement and initiation of the general resurrection.

As has been said, the most important event in life is death. We live to die and then we die to live. Mortality is very important, but no length of mortal life would be satisfactory if that life were not eternal. No one would want to live forever in the flesh. Death is our final graduation into eternal life.

If a body of flesh and bones were not necessary for eternity, then the resurrection would never have been initiated. And if a body of flesh and bones were not necessary for God the Father, then why would God the Son have been resurrected?

4

Bereavement

Every day death touches every facet of our lives and is probably the one event in life for which we should make the most study and the greatest preparation. We sometimes think of death as unpleasant; and because we usually don't like to think of unpleasant things, we may close our minds and turn away our faces when death approaches. But death does not cease to exist just because it is ignored.

The ancient Egyptians had a much more logical way of dealing with this situation when, on their great festive occasions, they kept constantly on display before the revelers a great image of death. Thus they continually held up this idea to impress everyone that someday everyone must die, that everyone who is born owes himself and God a death.

Someone has pointed out that, judging from the past, very few of us will get out of this world alive. From the time of his conception, every human being is living constantly under a death sentence waiting only for the verdict to be carried out. An inscription on one man's tombstone said, "I knew it would happen." This long, advance notice has been given to us that we might have time to adequately prepare for death.

But death has a great importance in addition to that which it has for itself alone. Every person is influenced by the death of every other person. Our greatest human concepts have to do with the immortality of the personality and the eternal glory of the human soul.

Recently I reread a Grecian tragedy written around the fall of Athens. In this tragedy a Roman general captured an Athenian philosopher, and he told the Athenian that he meant to put him to death. When the Athenian seemed little disturbed, the Roman thought he probably did not understand. And he told the Athenian that maybe he did not know what it meant to die.

Since the Athenian thought he understood death better than the Roman did, he told the Roman, "Thou dos't not know what it means to die for thou dos't not know what it means to live. To die is to begin to live. It is to end all stale and weary work, to begin a nobler and a better life. It is to leave deceitful knaves for the society of Gods and goodness.''

Death is a chief factor in our family relationships which causes a continual turnover in our leadership and a continual change in our attitude toward life. Much of our literature is born out of our attitudes toward our death. Many of our finest expressions of love and tribute are borne at our funerals. In fact, one of the most inspirational public meetings which we may attend is the funeral.

On November 27, 1975, during a break in the programmed General Authority meeting, a good friend of mine, ElRay L. Christiansen, put his hand on mine and said, ''Sterling, will you do something for me?''

I indicated that I would be delighted, if I could.

He said, ''When I die, I would like you to go to my casket, take me by the hand, and offer a prayer in behalf of myself and my family, and wish me Godspeed in the journey I will just then be beginning into immortality.''

He said, ''I do not know where I will be at that time, but I will be around; and I will know about it and will appreciate your interests in the welfare of myself and those that are near and dear to me.''

After his death a few days later, I was appointed to be on the committee that arranged the program for his funeral. Members of the committee went to his home to talk to his family about the arrangements they wished made. During this visit, I told his wife what ElRay had said. She answered, ''I hope you will do just as he requested.''

At a private viewing held later, I met her at the casket. I said, ''Louella, I think I will fulfill my promise to ElRay in a kind of symbolic way.''

She said, ''No, I think you should carry it out just as he requested.''

And so I put my hand on his and offered a prayer, which included my own expression of love for this great man who had been my devoted friend for over a quarter of a century. And since that time, I have thought about a funeral as a very pleasant way to honor greatness and friendship, and to bid an earthly farewell to those we love.

What tremendous significance is contained in the statement of Jesus himself when He said,

''. . . I am the resurrection, and the life: he that believeth in me, though he were dead, yet shall he live:

''And whosoever liveth and believeth in me shall never die.'' (John 11:25-26.)

The Lord has said, ''Thou shalt live together in love, insomuch that thou shalt weep for the loss of them that die, and more especially for those that have not hope of a glorious resurrection'' (D&C 42:45).

Death is an inescapable necessity in God's program for our eternal exaltation. The purposes of mortality may be accomplished in a few years of life. But when our bodies get old and cause us pain, God has provided the wonderful transformation of resurrection.

On one occasion, near the end of his long life, former president John Quincy Adams, who was an ardent believer in the immortality of the soul, met a friend on the streets of Boston. His friend said, "Mr. Adams, how are you?"

The former president replied, "John Quincy Adams himself is quite well, thank you sir, quite well indeed. But the house in which he is living is becoming quite delapidated and is tottering on its foundations. Time and the seasons have almost destroyed it. Its roof is warped and worn out. Its walls are so shattered that they tremble in every breeze. The old tenement is becoming almost uninhabitable, and I think I shall have to move out of it quite soon. But John Quincy Adams himself is quite well, thank you sir, quite well indeed."

The scriptures as well as our own reason indicates that death is good and in our interests. Elizabeth Barrett Browning wrote a sonnet to her husband which expressed her immortalized love for him. After enumerating some of the avenues her love had taken, she said:

> . . . I love thee with the breath,
> Smiles, (hopes and) tears, of all my life!—
> and, if God (wills)
> I shall but love thee better after death.

All of us who live at our best in this life shall love God, our friends, and our lives better after death.

Death involves all the events of life. Harry Emerson Fosdick once said:

"If the death of the body forever ended all there is of human life and personality, then the universe would be throwing away with utter heedlessness its most precious possession. A reasonable person does not even build a violin with infinite care, gathering the materials and shaping the body of it so that it can play the compositions of the masters, and then by some whim of chance-caprice smash it to bits. Neither does God create the great masterpiece of human life, and then, when it has just begun to live, throw it utterly away."

Certainly God, the all-wise and all-powerful Creator, did not build the stairway of human life to lead nowhere. It is an almost universal hope that all of us will love life, God, and each other better after death when we are resurrected, glorified, and eternalized with quickened senses, amplified powers of perception, and vastly increased capacity for love, understanding, success, and happiness.

Certainly death does not concern only those of advanced years. Many young people die, and we ought to know how to deal with the resulting bereavement.

Some time ago a father and mother who had lost a beautiful little three-year-old daughter through death came into my office seeking comfort. This man and his wife were parents of three children, ages five, three and one. The family was together in the living room where the children were playing when, with no warning, the little three-year-old just toppled over dead.

Of course the parents were heartbroken. I tried to sympathize with them as much as I could, but sympathy was not a very high compensation for their loss. I pointed out to them the promise of the Savior that those who die before the age of accountability, as this little girl had done, were assured of an eternal life in the highest, or celestial, kingdom of God (D&C 137:10).

But in her grief the mother seemed unimpressed. She pointed out that their little girl's mortal life had ended almost before it had begun, and that nothing could be worse. She made this statement several times, and each time her grief seemed to intensify.

Finally I said, "Sister Jones, I can understand your sorrow, but you have said nothing could be worse than the death of this beautiful, intelligent child at this age. I do not know whether it would help assuage your grief, but if you think it would help, I think I can tell you something that would be worse."

After she indicated that might be a consoling help, I told these broken-hearted parents about James Whitcombe Riley's poem, "Bereaved," which is not about the bereavement of a woman who lost a beautiful daughter but about the bereavement of one who had no child to lose:

> Let me come in where you sit weeping,—aye,
> Let me, who have (no) . . . child to die,
> Weep with you for the (loss of that) little one whose love
> I have known nothing of.

> (Let me imagine those) little arms that slowly, slowly loosed
> Their pressure round your neck; (those) hands you used
> To kiss. Such arms, such hands I never knew.
> (For them will you not let me come and weep with you?)
> (Out of an empty heart it may be that I could say something)
> Between the tears, that would be comforting—
> (For) ah! how sadder than (yourself) am I,
> (Who weep alone because I had no child to die.)

Even this distraught mother thought her grief would be small indeed compared to the bereavement described by the poet, Riley.

This mother had a memory that her childless sister did not have. She also had the assurance that this little child, though dead, would live again throughout eternity under the most ideal circumstances. When this woman recovered from the grief of her loss, she would realize that her little daughter was still hers, and she would still be there to inspire her life with joy.

I told this mother about my two little sisters who died of diptheria. One was age one, the other age seven. And I told her about the doctrine the Prophet Joseph Smith taught; that the infant child laid away in death would come up in the resurrection as a child; and, pointing to the mother of a lifeless child, he said to her, "You will have the joy, the pleasure, and satisfaction of nurturing this child, after its resurrection, until it reaches the full stature of its spirit" (*Gospel Doctrine,* pp. 455-456). This will apply to this woman's beautiful three-year-old child as well as my two little sisters who also died when very young.

There is restitution, there is growth, there is development after the resurrection from death. This doctrine speaks volumes of love, happiness, joy, and gratitude to our souls, and we should understand that, in the words of the Prophet Joseph Smith, "The (main) difference between the old and young dying is, one lives longer in heaven (the spirit world) and eternal light and glory than the other, and is freed a little sooner from this miserable, wicked world" (*Teachings of the Prophet Joseph Smith,* p. 197).

I had some wonderful experiences with my little seven-year-old sister who frequently went with me to milk the cows and do other farmyard chores. I love to think of her now as I read the scriptures about the resurrection and the glory of God that will belong to her as a natural right. And I love to think what this beautiful little sister will be like when I meet her again in heaven. I also like to repeat to myself some of these beautiful poems of bereavement as I think of her and her little sister and our mother and the other departed members of my family.

Everyone has many experiences with death that have great good as a consequence. Recently some strangers called and asked if they could come and talk with me about a serious tragedy that had taken place in their family, wherein their only daughter had just met her death under the wheels of a speeding automobile. They asked me if I would help them understand something about the purpose of life, the meaning of death, and what their relationship ought to be with each other.

They wanted to know if there *was* a God, if there *was* an eternal life, and if there *was* any reason for them to try to live on. So oppressive was this great calamity in their lives, it seemed as though they were smothering, that they could not breathe; and for two and a half hours I tried as hard as I could to help them with their problem. But there was not very much I could do because there was no place to begin.

It was not that these people particularly disbelieved in God. Up to that point in their lives, they just hadn't thought about Him one way or the other. Nor was it that they particularly disbelieved in eternal life. Up to that point, they hadn't really cared. But then death had stepped across that threshold and taken the best-loved personality there. And suddenly, right now, they needed to have great faith in God and they couldn't find it. You can't just snap your fingers and get great faith in God any more than you can snap your fingers and get great musical ability or acquire great financial skill.

This incident of death brings us face to face with the idea that, when we want a great ability or a great power, we must provide for it in advance. If we want to be a great doctor at age 46, we had better start to study at about age 6. And if we want to be prepared for the celestial kingdom in twenty years, it might be a good idea to start working on it now.

The best way to become a great soul in heaven is to be a great soul here. And the funeral, as well as our private meditations, and the conversations we have about death and about the hereafter may help us to prepare for the greater life that lies beyond the present.

5

The Poetry Of Bereavement

A number of years ago, a New York psychiatrist by the name of Smiley Blanton wrote a classic entitled *The Healing Power of Poetry*. For a period of forty years he used great ideas, many of them in poetic form, to help his patients deal successfully with their mental and emotional problems. This psychiatrist emphasized the fact that one of our greatest resources is our language, made of some 500,000 individual words, each invested with unique power for anyone who learns to use them effectively.

There was once a physician living in Birmingham, Alabama, who wrote prescriptions for people to be filled not at drugstores but at bookstores. This physician knew that the most valuable healing power is not found in bottles but in books; that heaven is not brought about by the use of wonder drugs but by the practice of wonderful ideas and activities.

Many of our outstanding authors have been poets. Someone has said that poetry is language dressed up in its best clothes. In poetry, every word is important and fits a particular place. Poetry is made of a language where the words have been especially selected, weighed, measured, colored, metered, rhymed, given a cadence, a mission, and sometimes set to music.

There is a poetry of courage. One may feel stronger after an idea filled with courage has been run through his mind and heart. There is a poetry of enthusiasm, a poetry of faith, a poetry of love, and a poetry of war. There is a poetry that can heal a broken heart and bestow upon a life a quality of peace and happiness that is almost miraculous.

Have you ever noticed the hush that comes over an audience when an appropriate poem is recited so that we rise above our ordinary language? This hush can be particularly noticeable at the funeral of a great human being.

However, death sometimes produces a devastating sorrow in the lives of those it touches. One of our most vital needs is to generate sufficient understanding and courage to learn how to most effectively handle these situations.

Many people are able to face the prospect of their own coming death with equanimity, and yet these same people may be unable to bear the shock of bereavement. The grief and misery of bereavement is something few people can imagine until the experience is upon them.

Therefore, it becomes a matter of great wisdom to prepare for the possibility that loved ones or particular friends may die at any time. We should build up an understanding of death so that when a loved one is taken we need not be left completely disconsolate and empty-handed.

This problem of bereavement has been with us since the beginning, and some ways of dealing with it are more satisfactory than others. We may seek consolation from the Word of the Lord as found in the Holy Scriptures. Nothing is more plainly written than the fact that the life of Christ did not begin at Bethlehem, neither did it end on Calvary. Jesus said, "I came forth from the Father, and am come into the world: again, I leave the world, and go to the Father" (John 16:28). We can be just as certain that our lives did not begin when we were born, nor will they end when we die.

After His resurrection, Jesus appeared in the midst of His disciples and said, ". . . Peace be unto you" (Luke 24:36). Again, He said, "Behold my hands and my feet, that it is I myself: handle me, and see; for a spirit hath not flesh and bones, as ye see me have" (Luke 24:39).

And He said:

". . . Have ye here any meat?

"And they gave him a piece of a broiled fish, and of an honeycomb.

"And he took it, and did eat before them." (Luke 24:41-43.)

Think how the emotions of those concerned must have been uplifted by His words. The record says:

"And the graves were opened; and many bodies of the saints which slept arose,

"And came out of the graves after his resurrection, and went into the holy city, and appeared unto many." (Matt. 17:52, 53.)

These were real people with real bodies. One of the most prominent teachings of the Holy Scriptures is that death is good. We know that Jesus lived as a member of the Godhead in His ante-mortal estate. The Lord said, ". . . Worlds without number have I created; and I also created them for mine own purpose; and by the Son I created them, which is mine Only Begotten" (Moses 1:33).

Of His own accord, Jesus accepted the nomination of His Eternal Heavenly Father to enter mortality and walk the dusty roads of Palestine, rather than rule in the presence of God, the Father, in heaven, to be born in the manger in Bethlehem, and to do the other things connected with birth and growing up just as we ourselves did. Like us, He was born under the death sentence. He said,

"... I lay down my life, that I might take it again.

"No man taketh it from me, but I lay it down of myself. I have power to lay it down, and I have power to take it again. . . ." (John 10:17-18.)

Upon the cross, His spirit and body were separated. He became the first fruits of the resurrection where His spirit and body were inseparably connected to make Him eligible for a fullness of joy. He did not return to the unembodied situation in which He lived during the Grand Council in Heaven. He changed His godly estate in heaven for what was temporarily a more humble estate in mortality with the same promise we have; that our mortal bodies may be resurrected without the frailties of flesh while having all the joys and adventure of the celestial kingdom.

If death is not good, certainly the Son of God, with full knowledge of that fact, would not have changed His situation for a chance to live in our mortality upon a telestial earth. Everyone should have a Bible concordance which would point out passages about each situation that may be faced, not only in the ante-mortal life, but in our second estate, as well as our post-mortal eternal lives.

We have a wonderfully consoling and stimulating poetry of bereavement which supplements truths of the hereafter as given in the Holy Scriptures. We also have some quotes on bereavement from our literature.

At age 83, as Victor Hugo approached the end of his life, he countered some possible skepticism by saying:

"You say the soul is nothing but the resultant of my bodily powers. Why then is my soul more luminous when my bodily powers begin to fail. Winter is on my head, but eternal spring is in my heart. I breathe at this hour the fragrance of the lilacs, the violets, and the roses as at 20 years.

"The nearer I approach the end, the plainer I hear around me the immortal symphonies of the world which invites me. It is marvelous, yet simple. It is a fairy tale, yet it is history.

"For half a century I have been writing my thoughts in prose, verse, history, satire, ode and song. I have tried all, yet I feel I have not said a thousandth part of what is in me.

"When I go down into my grave, I can say like many others, I have finished my day's work, but I cannot say I have finished my life. My day's work will begin again on the next morning.

"Death is not a blind alley, it is a thoroughfare; it closes upon the twilight. It opens upon the dawn."

At another time he said, "Let us not forget and let us teach it to all that there would be no dignity, that it would not be worthwhile to live if annihilation were to be our lot. What is it that alleviates, that renders men strong, wise, just, at once humble and aspiring, but the perpetual vision of a better world whose light shines through the darkness of the present life. As for myself, I believe profoundly in that better world, and after much struggle, many hardships, and numerous trials, this is the supreme conviction of my reason as it is the supreme consolation of my soul.''

An unknown poet said,

> He is not dead, my friend's not dead
> But, in the path we mortals tread,
> Has gone some few, trifling steps ahead
> And nearer to the end, so that you, too,
> Once past the bend
> Shall meet again as face to face
> This friend you fancied dead.

John L. McCreary wrote stimulating similar verse entitled ''There Is No Death.''

> There is no death! The stars go down
> To rise upon some fairer shore;
> And bright, in heaven's jeweled crown
> They shine forever more.
>
> There is no death! The dust we tread
> Shall change beneath the summer showers
> To golden grain or mellow fruit,
> Or rainbow-tinted flowers.
>
> The granite rocks disorganize,
> And feed the hungry moss they bear;
> The forest-leaves drink daily life
> From out the viewless air.
>
> There is no death! An angel-form
> Walks o'er the earth with silent tread;
> And bears our best-loved things away,
> And then we call them ''dead.''
>
> He leaves our hearts all desolate,
> He plucks our fairest, sweetest flowers;
> Transplanted into bliss, they now
> Adorn immortal bowers.
>
> The friendly voice, whose joyous tones
> Made glad these scenes of sin and strife,
> Sings now an everlasting song
> Around the tree of life.
>
> Where'er he sees a smile too bright
> Or heart too pure for taint and vice,
> He bears it to that world of light
> To dwell in Paradise.

Born unto that undying life,
They leave us but to come again
With joy we welcome them the same,
Except their sin and pain.

And ever near us, though unseen,
The dear immortal spirits tread;
For all the boundless universe
Is life—there are no dead!

Frequently a large part of our bereavement comes from the fact that we dwell on our own shortcomings and punish ourselves because we have not been as thoughtful as we should have been while the loved one was alive. We must learn to forgive ourselves as our loved ones in another world would surely forgive us.

William Cullen Bryant gives us a comforting faith in God in his "Ode to the Water Fowl" when he pictures this bird of passage seeking its southern home as winter approaches. We see him as a mere speck, solitary and alone, as he appears upon the northern horizon. His companions have gone on before. The closer he comes, the larger he seems to become. Finally, he rests momentarily to refresh himself with drink, then he takes to the air again, growing smaller and smaller, until he finally disappears over the southern horizon. Mr. Bryant finishes his verse with these thrilling words:

Thou art gone, the abyss of heaven
Hath swallowed up thy form, but on my heart
Deeply hath sunk this lesson thou hast given
And will not soon depart

He who from zone to zone
Guides through the boundless skies thy certain flight
In the long way that I must go alone
Will lead my steps aright.

Another author has given an interesting analogy of this transition of death when he said:

"I am standing upon the seashore. A ship at my side spreads her white sails to the morning breeze and starts for the blue ocean.

"She is a magnificent object of beauty and strength, and I stand and watch her until, at length, she hangs on the horizon like a speck of white cloud where the sea and the sky come together to mingle with each other. Then someone at my side whispers and says, 'There, she is gone.'

"Gone where? Gone from my sight, that is all. She is just as large in mast and hull and spar as she was when she first left my side, and just as able to bear her load of living weight to the place of her destination. Her diminished size is in me, not in her; and just at the moment when someone at my side whispers 'There, she is gone,' there are other eyes watching her coming, and other voices ready to take up the glad shout, saying, 'See, here she comes'—and such is dying.''

And another interesting contemplation is voiced by an unknown author who said:

> I cannot say and I will not say
> That she is dead. She is just away!
> With a cheery smile and a wave of her hand,
> She has journeyed into an unknown land.
>
> And left us dreaming, how very fair
> It needs must be, since she is there;
> And you—oh, you, who love and yearn
> For the old time step and the glad return.
>
> Think of her faring on, as dear
> In the love of there, as the love of here
> Mild and gentle as she was brave
> And the sweetest love of her life she gave
>
> To simple things; where the violet grew
> Pure as the eyes they were likened to.
> Loving service her hands have made
> As reverently as her lips have prayed.
>
> The little brown thrush that harshly stirred
> Was as dear to her as the mockingbird,
> And she pitied as much as her own in pain
> A writhing honey-bee wet with rain.
>
> Think of her still as the same, I say,
> She is not dead—she is just away.

The possibility of death should teach us not to neglect our friends and loved ones during this life. Someone wrote a helpful poem on this subject entitled "Around the Corner":

> Around the corner I had a friend
> In this great city that has no end.
> And the days went by and the weeks came on
> And before I know it a year is gone,
> And I never see my old friend's face,
> For life is a swift and terrible race.
> He knows I love him just as well
> As in the days when I rang his bell
> And he rang mine. We were youngsters then
> But now we're busy, tired men.

Tired of playing a foolish game,
Tired of trying to make a name.
Tomorrow, I say, I'll call on Jim
Just to show that I'm thinking of him.
But tomorrow comes and tomorrow goes
And the distance between us grows and grows.
Around the corner yet far away.
"Here's a telegram sir." Jim died today.
And that's what we get and deserve in the end,
Around the corner, a vanished friend.

In our bereavement we might say to ourselves, "Be strong and of a good courage; be not afraid, neither be thou dismayed; for the Lord thy God is with thee whithersoever thou goest" (Josh. 1:9).

6

Some Profound Observations About Life and Death

1. I never say that death is untimely because I never know.

2. Life is a mission and not a career.

3. Dr. Henry Eyring was once asked whether he thought there was a conflict between science and religion. He said, "I don't think there is any conflict between science and religion in God's mind."

4. William James said, "The best argument for an immortal life is the existence of a person who deserves one. But there are also some other good arguments for an eternal life. One is that God has promised that there will be one. He has also planted an eternal hope in every human breast that there will be one."

5. A mother lost two little daughters, one three years old and one five, within a week of each other. She said, "I love to think of my little children, whom God has called to Himself, as away at school—at the best school in the universe, under the best teachers, learning the best things in the best possible manner."

Such beautiful thoughts held in the mind over a long period will have a soothing, healing effect. Comforting ideas are as oil poured upon troubled waters. Time itself is a great healer.

6. During his last illness, a good man was asked whether he thought himself dying. He replied, "Really, my friend, it does not matter whether I am dying or not, for if I die, I shall be with God, and if I live, He will be with me."

7. Tryon Edwards said, "This world is the land of the dying, the next is the land of the living." The Holy Scriptures, supplemented by our reason, teach us that surely life in eternity will be more pleasant than it is in this veil of tears.

8. N. Macleod said, "We sometimes picture death as coming to destroy, whereas we should picture Christ as coming to save. We think of death as an ending, let us rather think of it as a new beginning. We think of losing, let us think of gaining. We think of parting, let us think of meeting again. We think of going away, let us think of arriving; and as the voice

of death whispers, 'You must go from earth,' let us hear the voice of Christ saying, 'You are coming to me.' "

9. John Milton said, "Death is the golden key that opens the palace of eternity."

10. Henry Ward Beecher said, "On this side of the grave we are strangers, on that citizens; on this side orphans, on that, children; on this side, captives, on that, free men; on this side, the disguised and unknown, on that, disclosed and proclaimed as the sons of God."

11. Joseph Smith said, "All of your losses will be made up to you in the resurrection, provided you continue faithful. By the vision of the Almighty I have seen it. (*History of the Church*, Vol. 5, p. 262.)

12. If the Savior could restore withered hands and straighten out crooked bodies and give sight to eyes that had never seen, certainly God can fulfill His promise of a resurrection and eternal glory.

13. Daniel Webster said, "The greatest thought that can ever enter the mind of any man is the consciousness of his individual relationship and responsibility to God."

14. When we pray, we talk to God. When we read the right things, He talks to us.

15. We sing an inspiring song in which we say, "I Walked Today Where Jesus Walked." Wouldn't it be a thrilling experience if, on some beautiful day, we could stand on that spot of ground where Jesus stood while we tried to reabsorb the spirit of His life? This action may not be practical for everyone, but there are actions that are practical, and even more important. We can think today what Jesus thought. We can read and absorb His every idea. We can live as He lived. We can do as He did. We can be what He wants us to become by doing what He wants us to do.

16. The scriptures say that, in the program of God, death itself will be done away with. Through John, in Revelations, He said, "And God shall wipe away all tears from their eyes; and there shall be no more death, neither sorrow, nor crying, neither shall there be any more pain: for the former things are passed away" (Rev. 21:4).

17. Weeping may endure for a night, but joy cometh in the morning.

18. The Greek hero, Ulysses, spent ten years fighting in the Trojan War. He spent an additional ten years crossing the three hundred miles of island-dotted sea to his homeland in Ithaca, Greece. By the time he arrived home, he was an old man. He had passed the retirement age for kings. Therefore, he put the crown upon the head of his son, placed the scepter in his son's hands, and set out on a new adventure. Tennyson has him say:

> How dull it is to pause, to make an end,
> To rust unburnished, not to shine in use.
> It's not too late to seek a better world

My purpose holds, to sail beyond the sunset
And the baths of all the western stars
Until I die. It may be that the gulf will wash us down.
It may be that we shall touch the happy isles,
And see the great Achilles whom we knew.
Though much is taken, much abides,
And though we have not now that strength
Which in old days moved earth and heaven,
Yet what we are, we are.
One equal temper of heroic hearts
Made weak by time and fate, but strong in will.
To strive, to seek, to find, and not to yield.

19.   We serve no God whose work is done
Who rests within his firmament
Our God his work has just begun
Toils evermore with powers unspent.

20.   Whistler's Mother:
And now, as evening shadows gather
About to fade off into gloom,
The mother sits alone, pose serene, husband gone,
      children gone, the work is done, twilight comes.
She thinks of the past in gratitude,
And gazes wistfully out into the future, unafraid.

This is a tribute every well-born son would like to pay to the mother who loved him into being, whose loving arms sustained him, whose unfaltering faith and appreciation encouraged him to do and to become. She was his wisest critic, his best friend, his mother.

21. After John the Revelator had seen the resurrection in vision, he said, "Blessed and holy is he that hath part in the first resurrection: on such the second death hath no power, but they shall be priests of God and of Christ, and shall reign with him a thousand years" (Rev. 20:6).

22. Life:

Life! We've been long together
Through pleasant and through cloudy weather
'Tis hard to part when friends are dear,
Perhaps it will cost a sigh, a tear;
Then steal away, give little warning,
Choose thine own time,
Say not goodnight, but in some brighter clime
Bid me "good morning."

                                        Anna L. Barbauld

23. In the *Improvement Era* for 1904, President Joseph F. Smith wrote an editorial on the resurrection of children. He said, "The body will come forth as it is laid to rest for there is no bodily growth or development in the grave. As it is laid down, so will it arise, and changes to perfection will come by the law of restitution. But the spirit will continue to expand and develop, and the body, after the resurrection, will develop to the full stature of man.

"This may be accepted as the doctrine of the Church in respect to the resurrection of children and their future development to the full stature of men and women; and it is alike conformable to that which will be regarded as both reasonable and desirable." (*History of the Church,* Vol. 4, pp. 556-557.)

24. God made a promise of a universal resurrection which He has continually reaffirmed through the prophets:

A. Job said, "For I know that my redeemer liveth . . ." (Job 19:25).

B. David said, "But God will redeem my soul from the power of the grave . . ." (Psalms 49:15).

C. Isaiah said, "Thy dead men shall live, together with my dead body shall they arise . . ." (Isaiah 26:19).

D. Daniel said, "And many of them that sleep in the dust of the earth shall awake, some to everlasting life, and some to shame and everlasting contempt" (Daniel 12:2).

25. Alexander Pope said, "Seeing we are here but for a day's abode, we must look elsewhere for an everlasting dwelling place where eternity is the measure, felicity the state, angels are the company, the Lamb is the light, and God is the portion and inheritance."

26. Tennyson said, "I am a part of all that I have met."

27. Emerson said, "I can no more remember the books I have read than the meals I have eaten, yet each is a part of all that I am."

28. We live a little,
    We love a little,
    We laugh a little,
    And then life is done.

29. The most important power in the world is the power of example. Carlyle said, "We reform others when we walk uprightly."

30. There is much more kindness than is ever spoken. The whole human family is bathed in an element of love like a mist of ether. How many people do we meet to whom we scarcely speak, yet whom we honor and who also honor us? How many people do we meet in the street or sit with in church, whom, though silently, we warmly rejoice to be with?

31. Joseph Smith said, "If you could gaze into heaven for five minutes, you would know more than by reading all that was ever written on the subject." We can also get some interesting ideas by gazing into hell.

32. The young mother set her foot on the path of life.

"Is the way long? she asked.

And the guide said, "Yes. And the way is hard. And you will be old before you reach the end of it. But the end will be better than the beginning."

But the young mother was happy, and she would not believe that anything could be better than these years. So she played with her children, and gathered flowers for them along the way and bathed with them in the clear streams; and the young mother cried, "Nothing will ever be lovelier than this."

Then night came, and storm, and the path was dark, and the children shook with fear and cold, and the mother drew them close and covered them with her mantle, and the children said, "Mother, we are not afraid, for you are near, and no harm can come." And the mother said, "This is better than the brightness of day, for I have taught my children courage."

And the morning came, and there was a hill ahead, and the children climbed and grew weary, and the mother was weary, but at all times she said to the children, "A little patience and we are there." So the children climbed and when they reached the top they said, "Mother, we could not have done it without you."

And the mother, when she lay down that night, looked up at the stars and said, "This is a better day than the last, for my children have learned fortitude in the face of hardship. Yesterday I gave them courage. Today I have given them strength."

And the next day came and strange clouds which darkened the earth—clouds of war and hate and evil, and the children groped and stumbled, and the mother said, "Look up. Lift your eyes to the light." And the children looked and saw above the clouds and Everlasting Glory, and it guided them and brought them beyond the darkness. And that night the mother said, "This is the best day of all, for I have shown my children God."

And the days went on, and the weeks and the months and the years, and the mother grew old, and little, and bent. But her children were tall and strong, and walked with courage. And when the way was hard, they helped their mother; and when the way was rough, they lifted her; for she was as light as a feather, and at last they came to a hill, and beyond they could see a shining road and golden gates flung wide.

And the mother said, "I have reached the end of my journey. And now I know that the end is better than the beginning, for my children can walk alone, and their children after them." And the children said, "You will always walk with us, Mother, even when you have gone through the gates."

And they stood and watched her as she went alone, and the gates closed after her. And they said, "We cannot see her but she is with us still. A mother like ours is more than a memory. She is a living presence."

33. Mary Todd Lincoln passed away on July 15, 1882, at the age of 64, seventeen years after her husband's brutal murder. Reverend James G. Reed conducted the funeral service for Mary Lincoln. In his eulogy, he said that Abe and Mary Lincoln had been like two stately pine trees growing together

toward the sky. The branches of each were intermingled with the other; and on that fatal day of April 14, 1865, when one was stricken down by lightning, the other had been killed at the same time. However, Abe survived the shot for only one day while for years Mary endured a kind of living death.

34. "Blessed are the dead who die in the Lord" (D&C 63:49).

35. Thomas Curtis Clark said,

"I saw him once, he stood a moment there.
He spoke a word that laid his spirit bare.
He clasped my hand then passed beyond my ken,
But what I was I shall not be again."

36.

To every man upon this earth
Death cometh soon or late
And every man may give his life
To something good and great.

And how can man die better
Than in facing fearful odds
For the ashes of his fathers
And the temples of his gods.

37. H. A. Hamilton said, "I never think he is quite ready for another world who is altogether weary of this."

38. The Beyond:

It seemeth such a little way to me,
As cross to that strange country, the beyond;
And yet, no stranger, for it has grown to be
The home of those of whom I am so fond.

They make it seem familiar, and most dear,
As journeying friends bring distant countries near.
And so for me there is no sting at death,
And so the grave has lost its victory;

It is but crossing with abated breath
And white, set face, a little strip of sea,
To find the loved ones waiting on the shore,
More beautiful, more precious than before.

39.

A precious one from us is gone
The voice we loved is stilled
A place is vacant in our home
Which never can be filled

God in his wisdom has recalled
The boon his love has given
And though his body slumbers here
His soul is safe in heaven.

40. Dr. Wernher von Braun said, "Many people seem to feel that science has somehow made 'religious ideas' untimely or old-fashioned. But I think science has a real surprise for the skeptics. Science, for instance, tells us that nothing in nature, not even the tiniest particle, can disappear without a trace. Nature doesn't know extinction. All it knows is transformation.

"Now if God applies this fundamental principle to the most minute and insignificant parts of His universe, doesn't it make sense to assume that He applies it also to the human soul? I think it does. And everything science has taught me—and continues to teach me—strengthens my belief in the continuity of our spiritual existence after death. Nothing disappears without a trace."

41. The Builder:

The builder builded a temple,
He wrought it with grace and skill,
Pillars and groins and arches
All fashioned to work his will.
Men said as they saw its beauty.
"It shall never know decay;
Great is thy skill, O builder!
Thy fame shall endure for aye."

A teacher builded a temple
With loving and infinite care,
Planning each arch with patience,
Laying each stone with a prayer.
None praised his unceasing efforts
None knew of his wondrous plan,
For the temple the Teacher builded
Was unseen by the eyes of man.

Gone is the Builder's temple
Crumbled into the dust;
Low lies each stately pillar,
Food for consuming rust.
But the temple the Teacher builded
Will last while the ages roll,
For that beautiful unseen temple
Was a child's immortal soul.

42. Carry On:

>Things may not look well, but then you never can tell
>So carry on, old man, carry on.
>Be proud of your mission
>Greet life with a cheer
>Give it all that you've got
>That's why you are here
>Fight the good fight, and be true to the end
>And at last when you die
>Let this be your cry
>Carry on, my soul, carry on.

43.

>Sometime, when life's lessons have been learned,
>And the sun and stars forevermore have set,
>And the things which our weak judgments here have spurned,
>The things o'er which we grieved with lashes wet,
>Will flash before us out of life's dark night,
>As stars shine most in deeper tints of blue;
>And we shall see how all God's plans are right,
>And how what seemed reproof was love most true.

>And we shall see how, while we frown and sigh,
>God's plans go on as best for you and me;
>How, when we called, He heeded not our cry
>Because His wisdom to the end could see,
>And e'en as prudent parents disallow
>Too much of sweets to craving babyhood.
>So God, perhaps is keeping from us now
>Life's sweetest things, because it seemeth good.

>And you shall shortly know that lengthened breath
>Is not the sweetest gift God sends his friend,
>And that, sometimes, the sable pall of death
>Conceals the fairest bloom His love can send.
>If we could push ajar the gates of life,
>And stand within and all God's workings see,
>We could interpret all this doubt and strife,
>And for each mystery could find a key.

>But not today. Then be content, poor heart;
>God's plans, like lilies pure and white, unfold.
>We must not tear the close-shut leaves apart—
>Time will reveal the calyxes of gold,
>And if, through patient toil, we reach the land
>Where tired feet, with sandals loosed, may rest,

When we shall clearly see and understand
I think that we will say, "God knew the best."

May Riley Smith

44. When the great Scorer comes to mark against your name
He'll not write, "good" or "bad," but how you played the game.

Grantland Rice

45. John Wesley said, "Our men die well because they have previously lived well."

46. Out there lying on the field, I died a thousand deaths. But somehow we do not mind the crucifixion when we are sure of the resurrection.

47. Do not do away with the cross as a Christian symbol, but the cross is an empty cross, a cross from which the Lord of Life has gone. He is risen, the cross is deserted and left behind forever.

48. They thought that they had heard the last word from Jesus at the ninth hour of Good Friday but, in a much larger sense, that was actually just the beginning. Our Good Friday will also mark the beginning of the most important events in our lives. The resurrection has changed Easter from a depressing sunset to a glorious sunrise.

49.   Pain stayed so long, I said to him today
             I will not have you with me any more.
             I stomped my foot and said, be on your way
             Then paused there startled at the look he wore.

             I who have been your friend, said he to me,
             I who have been your teacher. All you know
             Of understanding, love and sympathy,
             Of patience I have taught you, shall I go?

             He spoke the truth, this strange, unwanted guest.
             I watched him leave and knew that he was wise.
             He left a heart made tender in my breast
             He left a clearer vision in my eyes.
             (I dried my tears and lifted up a song,
             Even for one who tortured me so long.)

50. Recently I saw an article in a magazine about a giant sequoia that had been struck by lightning. The growth rings of this giant tree, when counted, showed it to be over four thousand years old. The article said there was no evidence that any of these giant trees had ever died of natural causes. If a tree can live to be four thousand years old, what are the possibilities of a child of God?

51. President McKay frequently recited a poem called "Supposing." It said,

Supposing today was your last day on earth,
The last mile of your journey you'd trod.
After all of your struggles, how much are you worth?
How much can you take home to God?

Don't count as possessions your silver and gold,
For tomorrow you leave them behind,
And all that is yours to have and to hold
Are the blessings you've given mankind.

Just what have you done as you've journeyed along
That is really and truly worthwhile?
Do you think that your good deeds would offset the wrong?
Can you look o'er (your) life with a smile?

We are only supposing, but if it were real
And you invoice your deeds from your birth
And figure the profits you made in life's deal,
How much are you really worth?

52. Something Out Of Nothing: We accuse some Christians of teaching false doctrines when they say God made the earth out of nothing. We say that is impossible, that even God can't make something out of nothing.

In the beginning God said to those who were associated with Him in the creation, "We will go down for there is space there, and we will take of these materials, and we will make an earth whereon these may dwell;

"And we will prove them herewith, to see if they will do all things whatsoever the Lord their God shall command them." (Abraham 3:24-25.)

But frequently we preach a much more serious false doctrine when we say that we can make success and happiness out of nothing. You can't make successful leadership out of nothing. You can't make faith out of nothing. You can't make happiness out of nothing. Certainly we can't make eternal life out of nothing. We make success out of righteousness and industry and planning and enthusiasm. We make eternal life out of ambition and obedience to God and a determination to succeed. The more high grade the ingredients are with which we work, the more glorious will be our eternal life.

53.   When the high heart we magnify
And the sure vision celebrate
And worship greatness passing by
Ourselves are great.

7

A Review Of Life and
A Preview Of Death

A great many of life's situations come in pairs. If we want to clearly understand one, it may be helpful to find out as much as possible about the other. To understand the great experience of death, we need to know as much as possible about life.

By the time we were ready to make the transition into this life, we had come to a place where young people always come, where it was desirable for us to move away from the homes of our parents, where we could learn to stand on our own feet and establish a home of our own. God wanted us to move away from His presence because no sin is permitted where God is, and He wanted us to see good and evil side by side. He wanted us to learn right from wrong and to develop the character to select the right.

This life is the place where we would be tested and proven and tried. Mortality is very important, but it was never intended to be more than a temporary condition to prepare us for the greater life which lies beyond, where we may have glory added upon our heads forever and ever.

It has been reported that when one stands in the presence of imminent death, a panorama of his life passes before him. However, if this preview of death is done early enough, it may increase the quality of our lives, both here and hereafter. It seems unfortunate that we do not take sufficient advantage of this reviewing and previewing procedure at regular intervals throughout our lives, rather than waiting for the end of life or some present crisis that we cannot do very much about.

Someone has said the greatest gift God has given to man is an imagination. Since we do have this ability to think constructively about things before they happen, we can learn the most important lessons of life in advance. We can also relive experiences of our past, and by this process we can reabsorb the original good so that we may gain the strength that will prepare us for the problems of life that lie ahead.

As an illustration of this important idea, there is a paragraph in President McKay's book, *Gospel Ideals,* in which he says, "Last night I dreamed about my mother." And then he said, "I would like to dream about my mother more often." That is, in his dream he went back and relived those important days at his mother's knee, when he learned the lessons of life that brought him to his ultimate high place.

President McKay did not learn how to be the President of the Church when he was ninety or eighty or seventy. He learned those lessons when he was five and ten and fifteen years of age while still under the direction of his mother. And then, long after his mother had passed away, he would go back and relive those important experiences in his dream so that when he awakened in the morning he had that additional strength as though he had actually had this stimulating learning experience with his mother during the night.

But one does not need to be asleep in order to dream. Neither are thinking processes limited to the present. The productive power of our minds can go backward or forward across time or space more quickly than we can leave a room. We can produce strength by *re*living life, and we can find greater direction by *pre*living death; and we may absorb strength from both directions.

It is important that we think about birth and the life that follows it. We should also think about death and the life that follows it. Death is the most important event in life. As birth is our graduation from our ante-mortal state, so death is our graduation into eternal life.

While I do not want to unduly frighten anyone, I would like to point out as gently and as kindly as I can that someday each one of us is going to die, and we had better be ready. When we clearly understand that death is an indispensable part of our program, we can prepare for it more intelligently. Death is our only gateway into immortality.

We can make eternity more pleasant by thinking about death in advance so that we can be prepared in our righteousness when it arrives. Every day we are marching toward death, but only the last day brings us to it.

The purpose of the gospel, and the purpose of life itself, is to teach us how to live eternally. And the death hour is the key hour which judges all other hours. No one can tell whether his life has been successful or not until his last hour. That is, you could not write the life story of Jesus of Nazareth or Judas Iscariot without knowing about their last hour. Sophocles said that just as one must wait until the evening to discover how pleasant the day had been, so one can really not judge life until death.

But we can make our lives better by thinking about each part of it in advance. For example, young people ought to prelive the day of their marriage. They should make decisions about that important time when they will kneel at the marriage altar before God in the presence of a very special person to make certain covenants that will endure the rest of their lives.

I would like to tell you the story of two people who lived in their last hour. Probably neither of these experiences actually took place, yet they are just as true as if they had happened a million times, as indeed in principle they have.

One is the legendary story of Faust. You may remember that Dr. John Faust died in Wittenberg, Germany, in the year 1540. But twenty-four years before his death, he made a deal in which he sold his soul to Satan. He said to Satan, "If you will aid me for twenty-four years, punishing my enemies and aiding my friends, at the end of that period I will forever deliver up my soul."

Now that seemed like a good idea to Faust because twenty-four years is a long time, and the end of twenty-four years may never actually arrive. He thought, "What difference does it make anyway what happens after twenty-four years?" But Satan, with more perspective, said, "I will wait on Faustus while he lives, and he shall buy my service with his soul."

The twenty-four years began, and Faust had every experience of good and bad. But almost before he was aware, it was said to Faust, as it must be said to every one of us, "Thine hour is come." This was the first time Faust had ever thought about the possibility that he must pay the debt. And for the first time he knew how badly he had cheated himself. He now wanted desperately to change the agreement, but that was impossible. And so Faust prayed:

"Oh, God, if thou canst have no mercy on my soul, at least grant some end to my incessant pain. Let Faustus live in hell a thousand years, or even a hundred thousand, but at last be saved."

But Faust knew that, according to his own bargain, even this could never be. He sat and watched the clock tick off the seconds. Finally, just as the hour struck, Faust uttered these last words before he died: "Faustus is gone to hell." If Faust had lived in his imagination his last hour first, he never would have allowed himself to come to such an awful end.

The habit of living only in the present is what got Esau into trouble. You remember that night when Esau came home hungry and said to his brother, Jacob, "If you will give me your mess of pottage, I will sign over to you the birthright of all my lands and cattle, houses, barns, and crops." To one who had just had a good dinner that may not seem like a very good idea, but Esau was hungry. He probably thought, "What difference does it make what happens in ten years? I am hungry right now."

I do not even know what a mess of pottage is, nor does it sound very appetizing to me, but Esau traded off his entire birthright in order to get it. Every one of us makes some of those same mistakes when we trade a future birthright for a present mess of pottage.

I have a relative who has an interesting philosophy of reading. When she reads a novel, she always reads the last chapter first. She wants to know before she begins where she is going to be when she gets through. And that is a good idea for life.

Another man who lived in his last hour was the great Cardinal Wolsey, a contemporary of King Henry VIII. You may remember Shakespeare's character: He was very wealthy, he had great power, he had made and unmade kings and kingdoms. But along the way, thinking as most of us do that the end would never find him out, he had done evil; and in his last hour he found himself discovered, discredited, and discarded. His property was confiscated by the state, his robes withdrawn by the church, and in that humble place where he went to die he said in substance these words:

"The last hour of my long and weary life has come upon me. I have done not well, and may God have mercy on my soul. Farewell, a long farewell to all my greatness. This is the state of man; today he puts forth the tender leaves of hope, tomorrow blossoms and bears its blushing honors thick upon him. The third day comes the frost, the killing frost, and then he falls as I do, never to hope again. I have ventured many summers in the sea of glory, far beyond my depth. I have sounded all the depths and shoals of honor, but I have missed the way. My high-blown pride at last broke under me, and left me weary and old in service to the mercy of the rude stream."

Then he said to his servant, the only one who had not forsaken him:

"Oh, Cromwell, Cromwell, I charge thee, fling away ambition. By that sin the angels fell . . . corruption wins not more than honesty. Be just and fear not. Let all the ends thou aimest at be thy country's, thy God's, and truth's. Then if thou diest, thou diest a blessed martyr."

Then he said:

"Oh, Cromwell, Cromwell, had I but served my God with half the zeal I served my king, he would not in mine age have left me naked to mine enemies."

If the cardinal had lived his last hour first, he never would have come to this unpleasant end.

It is said that the Lord knows the end from the beginning. If we properly learn to preview our lives, this may also, to some extent, be said of us.

8

The Funeral

We have a wonderful custom among us of holding funerals. That is, when a friend or a loved one dies, family members and friends of the loved one are invited to meet at some sacred place, in the presence of the deceased, to hold a memorial service. The purpose of this service might be made up of three main sections.

1. We have the privilege of paying our tribute of love and devotion to the deceased.

2. We are offered an opportunity to comfort and console the bereaved.

3. We are afforded time for contemplation, for evaluation, and for some resolutions as to how we might better prepare our own lives for this event when it shall come to us.

When a memorial service is held, family members come from far and near, and a few intimate friends are bidden to participate in this constructive experience. So far as bringing families together is concerned, the function of the funeral might, in some ways, be comparable to the mission of Elijah assigned to him by the Lord when He said to the people,

"Behold, I will send you Elijah the prophet before the coming of the great and dreadful day of the Lord:

"And he shall turn the heart of the fathers to the children, and the heart of the children to their fathers, lest I come and smite the earth with a curse." (Mal. 4:5, 6.)

On the occasion of a funeral, our hearts reach out with as much love as we feel at any other time in our lives. At this important service, we hear inspiring music, listen to sacred prayers, meditate upon things of the spirit, and offer in our own hearts our personal tributes of love and respect to the deceased. A funeral is one of those infrequent occasions when we think seriously of God, the atonement of Christ, the resurrection, the celestial kingdom, and what our own lives ought to be when we, too, shall come to this time of transition.

Death does not change us from what we are; and, from some points of view, there is not much difference between life before and life after death. We might ask ourselves, "Who are the living but this comparatively small handful of people who presently occupy the earth on a temporary basis? And who are the dead but that vast throng whose bodies slumber in earth's bosom waiting for ours to join them?"

Many years ago, John Donne wrote his famous poem, "No Man Is An Island." Mr. Donne said,

> No man is an island,
> No man stands alone,
> Each man's joy is a joy to me
> Each man's grief is my own.
>
> We need one another,
> And I will defend
> Each man as my brother,
> Each man as my friend.

Later, in devotions upon emergent occasions, Mr. Donne wrote, "No man is an island, entire of itself; every man is a piece of the continent, a part of the main; if (any part of the continent) be washed away by the sea, (then every man is the loser by just that much;) . . . any man's death diminishes me, because I am involved in mankind; . . ."

Every man has a stake in every other man's accomplishments. Each man holds an interest in every man's deeds. When someone beautifies the landscape or invents a labor-saving device, all are enriched. When the tide comes in, all the ships in the harbor are lifted up. When someone improves the frontiers of his own mind or spirit, the general intellectual or spiritual level is raised. Likewise, when anyone dies, we are diminished, for a part of us has also passed away.

Based on Mr. Donne's poem, Ernest Hemmingway wrote his famous masterpiece, *For Whom the Bell Tolls.* He said, ". . . Therefore, who can say for whom the bell tolls? It tolls for the dead, but it tolls for all. It tolls for thee."

Life is not a game of solitaire. Nor is this memorial service just a funeral for the deceased. The whole family is involved, as well as the whole community, the whole church, the whole nation, and every individual in it. If the shortstop on the baseball team makes an error, the whole team may lose the game. If one football player is offside, all of his associates are penalized.

It is a bit ridiculous for us to say about the tragedy of another that it is his funeral, because it is also our funeral. We dare not ignore the needs of others, whether it be for their bodies, their minds, their souls, or their pocketbooks, because we are also more or less involved. To some extent, we all tend to rise or fall, sink or swim, together. We share in everyone's success.

Booms and panics spread themselves over the community. While Andrew Carnegie was becoming a millionaire, he made thirty-eight other men millionaires. When one man becomes an alcoholic or a bankrupt, he usually drags others along with him. When one climbs to spiritual or material heights, others are made better. We live a part of everyone's life, and we die a part of everyone's death. A common interest and a common destiny bind us together both here and hereafter.

As the Prophet Joseph Smith has informed us, if we do not seek out our dead, and do what we can in their interests, we imperil our own salvation. Much the same thing happens when we fail to be lifted up by each other. If the husband dies, it is also the wife's funeral because, with his death, many parts of her have also passed away.

Everyone ought to write his own autobiography, and he ought to write it in advance. It has been said that an autobiography is, in some ways, like a financial budget. There are some people whose budget consists of a mere written detail as to where the money went. There are other people who, by their advance budget planning, tell the money where to go. And our autobiographies are often like that. Frequently we wait until we die and then somebody else records what we did. A much better autobiography would be for us to thoroughly plan each year of our lives in advance, so that we can tell our lives where to go.

And it might be a good idea to prelive our own funeral and to figure out what kind of person we would like to have in the casket on the day we receive our last and highest honors. In that way, we might increase the possibilities for a more pleasant funeral.

Someone has said, "If you want a job done well, do it yourself." That would certainly apply to getting the excellence into our lives which would give someone something extraordinary to say in a eulogy which is dedicated to us.

We can put interest in all three of these departments by providing, for our own funeral, a deceased worthy of the highest tributes of love and respect, as well as the inspiration and example that we can provide for other people who will follow us. We can also comfort the bereaved by being men and women of great accomplishment so that the bereaved will not only be comforted, but will feel admiration and joy.

Only we can determine what kind of person we will be when this important funeral event shall happen to us.

9

The Eulogy

Life generally is made up of problems and difficulties. We have hardships to overcome and endure. But when life is ended and death comes, we lavish much praise on the one departing this life. Such a memorial service may be about the only opportunity some people will ever have in which to receive public acclaim. On this occasion, however, time and opportunity are made available to those who are interested in expressing private and personal commendation of the deceased's character, or to enumerate various services rendered.

On other occasions, we might use the trite expression we frequently hear when a group of individuals is being introduced to the audience. The presiding officer may say, "Will you please withhold your applause until all have been introduced."

During one's lifetime, we frequently adopt the spirit of saying, "Will you please withhold your applause until his funeral." But when the funeral actually takes place, then we seem to go all out in presenting the deceased with flowers, and we open the floodgates of praise for his many good deeds we see more clearly.

It used to irritate me to watch someone spend his life in the midst of arguments and problems, and then, when I attended his funeral, to hear nice things said about him, who in life would have thought them strange. However, I don't feel that way any more. I like to know people who spend time investigating the lives of others in order to say the most praiseworthy things possible about them. And I hope no one will ever hear me say, "withhold the applause."

Actually, there are no ordinary people. If we could understand the greatness of the life of any "ordinary" person, we may feel as if we should fall down to worship before them.

For example, if you could have seen Abraham as he tended his sheep out on the plains of Palestine, you may have thought of him as a rather ordinary kind of shepherd. But if you could have seen Abraham as he stood

among the noble and great in the council of God, or if you could look in on
Abraham at this instant as he serves God with all of his background char-
acteristics and great virtues exposed to view, you may have a completely
different attitude toward him.

Ralph Waldo Emerson once said that he had never met anyone who
was not his superior in some particular. I feel certain this is true of every
other person. That is, God gives each of us some talent or some personality
trait or some ability that we can develop whereby we are expected to set a
good example for everyone else in the world. Then, through our occupation, or avocation, our religious and family assignment, we may pool our
good qualities and use them for the benefit and uplift of each other.

Certainly our own funeral is one of the most important gatherings we
will ever attend. Even as spirits, it might be pleasant for us to hear some of
the nice things said about us by friends who have been appointed to participate in rites that will be the last ones we will ever receive upon this earth.

All of us are strangers in this world. We travel through life incognito,
knowing little about ourselves. Someone once said to his friend, "Who do
you think you are?" And the friend whispered quietly unto himself and
said, "I wish I knew."

We will all find someday that we are very important people. We will
discover the truth of what we have heard rumored; we are all children of
God, formed in His image and endowed with His talents and potentialities.
We are all natives of heaven. The Apostle Paul said we should be careful
how we entertain strangers because some have entertained angels unaware.

If we could turn the calendar back for our deceased friend to his ante-
mortal existence, we would probably find many wonderful things to his
credit with which we are presently unfamiliar, but for which he is entitled
to praise. Or if we could see our own lives clearly, we would probably discover many praiseworthy things we now know little or nothing about.

Sometimes the real purpose of our life is not understood, even by us.
It may have been that we were friends of Abraham and Moses in the ante-
mortal council of God. Very likely we also have a great future which we
ourselves may not even begin to comprehend. But whether our praise comes
from our accomplishments in the past or in the present, the eulogy is still an
important part of life and of death.

Certainly one of the most pleasant and necessary functions of a funeral,
both for the deceased as well as for loved ones and friends, is the eulogy.
Through the eulogy, we may offer some measure of comfort and consolation to the bereaved.

To mourn is natural; and since God makes no duplicates, there are no
substitutes for the deceased. We have only one mother and one father, and
no one can take the place assigned to someone else. But what a thrilling
opportunity is presented in the eulogy to point out both to the bereaved and

to ourselves the tremendous advantages and opportunities that lie beyond the boundaries of this life. Many new doors are opened in our minds and hearts by death.

A eulogy is an instrument used for teaching, comforting, appreciating, healing, and learning, with some beautiful thoughts of praise, appreciation, inspiration, and blessing with which we start someone on his way as he makes his departure from this tremendously important period of his second estate. Certainly the custom of giving a eulogy at the funeral of a great and noble person gives practice in our duties of laudation and commendation which should be more enthusiastically indulged throughout a person's life. Thus they will be in the proper form at the time of his death. This eulogy should begin early in life. We ought to praise our wives and children. We ought to praise our parents.

John Milton, in his great epic poem, "Paradise Lost," has Adam offer praise of our mother Eve:

> Grace was in all her steps and
>   heaven was in her eyes,
> In every gesture there was dignity and love.
> When I approach her loveliness, so absolute she seems
> And in herself complete.
> So well to know her own that what she wills to do or say
>   seems wisest, virtuest, discreetest, best.
> All higher knowledge in her presence falls degraded.
> Wisdom in discourse with her loses, discountenanced and
>   like folly shows.

Other expressions of commendation follow:

1. At his brother's funeral, Robert G. Ingersoll said, "If everyone to whom he did some loving service should bring a blossom to his grave, he would sleep tonight beneath a wilderness of flowers."

2. Shakespeare said, "His life was gentle and the elements so mixed in him that nature might stand up and say to all the world, 'Here was a man.' " Again he said, "Here was a man. Take him for all in all. I think I shall not look upon his like again."

3. Henry Wadsworth Longfellow said,

> Were a star quenched on high
>   For ages would its light
> Still traveling downward from the sky
>   Shine on our mortal sight
> So when a great man dies
>   For years beyond our ken
> The light he leaves behind him lies
>   Upon the paths of men.

An article in the *Readers Digest* sometime ago told of someone who placed a block of silver against a block of gold and left it there for two years. During this waiting period, the molecular action in each of these solids had thrown little flecks of itself across the boundary to be embedded in the other. When they were taken apart, flecks of silver were found in the gold and flecks of gold in the silver.

There is no place where such a molecular action can take place more effectively than in human personality. Each individual person is radio-active. Each is surrounded by an aura or atmosphere that is sending out little flecks of character, faith, and enthusiasm, which are being incarnated in all those who come within their broadcasting range.

10

Our Great Days

We have a constructive custom among us in which we set aside special days on which to think about special things. We set aside the second Sunday in May as Mother's Day, and on this day we let our minds reach up as we try to understand the purpose for which this day was set apart. The third Sunday in June is set apart as Father's Day for the same reason. Such a custom has value because the human mind has some of the qualities of the tendrils of a climbing vine as it tends to attach itself and draw itself upward by that with which it comes in contact.

Other special days can put our minds in contact with other important ideas. We have Memorial Day, Pioneer Day, and Easter. We have Christmas, and the Fourth of July. We set aside the fourth Thursday in November as Thanksgiving.

Another of our constructive customs is a memorial service to pay tribute to one recently deceased.

At one such service I felt honored to pay tribute to Leone Romney. I spoke of the three most important dates in the life of Leone Romney. The first one was November 7, 1894. That was the date that she was born. The second of these was June 15, 1915. That was the date that she was married. The third of these was March 20, 1976. That was the date when she died. To make the most of each of these dates, we might think about them individually.

Leone Romney was not born by accident. She earned the right to be born. One of the greatest accomplishments of her life was that she was well born into a wonderful lineage. However, Jesus said that one birth was not enough; that everyone ought to be born twice. And so on her baptismal date, Leone Romney was born of the water and of the spirit in the exact meaning of that term as indicated by Jesus.

She became a member of The Church of Jesus Christ of Latter-day Saints. All its great life-developing concepts were made an official part of the program of her life. She also had authorized hands laid upon her head for the reception of the Holy Ghost.

However, no one is limited to two births. Everyone can be born again as many times as he desires. Phillips Brooks was once asked when was he born, and he said, "It was one Sunday afternoon about 3:30 p.m. after I had just finished reading a great book." When one gets a great conviction into his heart, he is born again. When one is married, he acquires a new set of needs and becomes a different person.

Date number two in the life of Leone Romney was June 15, 1915. That was the day of her marriage to Orson Douglas Romney, Jr. And as she was well born, so was she well married. In imagination I would like to take you who are her posterity back a few years to a time antedating your birth. All of us could not be born at the same time, nor can all of us die at the same time. You knew long before you were born that you were going to have the privilege of coming here and receiving these beautiful, wonderful bodies of flesh and bone, without which you could never have a fulness of joy or accomplishment, either in this life or in the life to come.

How interested you children must have been in this marriage of Leone Hamblin and O. D. Romney, Jr. Everything in your life depended upon it, including the purity of your bloodstream, the quality of your mental power, and the instruction in life's purposes that you would receive. They were permitted to come here ahead of you to learn the lessons of life that would help you to make your lives successful. They were sent here to establish a family of which you could be proud. They were enabled to build a home in which you might be welcomed into this life.

Leone Romney has left the world a better place because she has passed through it. As I have been listening to these family histories, I have thought of the many millions of evidences there are in the world which indicate that Leone Romney has lived here. This world will forever be a better place because of her.

The third date in the big three of the life of Leone Romney was March 20, 1976. That was the date of her death. O. D. was called back home some twenty-five years before Leone, and for a quarter of a century she was left to carry on alone as the head of the family.

Albert Kenney Rowswell has written what might have been a pact between O. D. and Leone a quarter of a century ago when each said to the other,

> Should you go first and I remain
> To walk the road alone,
> I'll live in memory's garden, dear,
> With the happy days we've known.
> In spring I'll watch for roses red,
> When fades the lilac blue,
> In early Fall when brown leaves call
> I'll catch a glimpse of you.

Should you go first and I remain
    For battles to be fought,
Each thing you've touched along the way
    Will be a hallowed spot.
I'll hear your voice, I'll see your smile,
    Though blindly I may grope,
The memory of your helping hand
    Will buoy me up with hope.

Should you go first and I remain
    To finish with the scroll,
No length'ning shadows shall creep in
    To make this life seem droll.
We've known so much of happiness,
    We've had our cup of joy,
And memory is one gift of God
    That death cannot destroy.

Should you go first and I remain,
    One thing I'd have you do.
Walk slowly down that long, lone path,
    For soon I'll follow you.
I'll want to know each step you take
    That I may walk the same,
For some day down that lonely road
    You'll hear me call—your name.

Now Leone and O. D. will be permitted to again continue on together.

And so we meet here today to express our great love and appreciation for the lives of these two people who have meant so much to all of us. We might get help in improving the quality of our lives when we think about those important experiences that surely lie beyond our mortal boundaries.

Someone obviously had this in mind in the song, "Beyond the Sunset":

Beyond the sunset, Oh blissful morning
When, with our Saviour, heaven is begun,
Earth's toiling ended, oh glorious dawning,
Beyond the sunset when day is done.

Beyond the sunset, no clouds will gather,
No storms will threaten, no fears annoy.
Oh day of gladness, oh day unending,
Beyond the sunset, eternal joy.

Beyond the sunset, oh glad reunion
When with our dear loved ones who've gone before
In that fair homeland, we'll know no parting
Beyond the sunset, forevermore.

I would like to wish every member of this great family the success to which you are entitled by reason of your ante-mortal excellence by reason of your birth through this chosen lineage, and the destiny decreed for you. The ancients had a way of expressing their good wishes when they said:

May the road rise up to meet you.
May the wind be always at your back.
May the sun shine warm upon your face and the
rains fall gently on your fields.
And now and forever may God hold you lovingly
in the hollow of His hand.

The prophet Moses quoted the Lord as giving the religious version of this blessing when he said:

The Lord bless thee, and keep thee.
The Lord make his face shine upon thee,
and be gracious unto thee.
The Lord lift up his countenance upon thee,
and give thee peace. (Numbers 6:24-26.)

11

Funeral Orations

On December 30, 1981, I attended the funeral service for Henry Eyring, one of the greatest men, in my opinion, who has ever lived. He was honored worldwide as an eminent scientist, yet he was a man of humble faith who loved his family and friends and God. He was one of the most distinguished men I have ever known. What was said about Henry Eyring at his funeral, about God, and about the life of this man, was one of the finest expressions of truths I have ever heard.

Afterwards I thought of other statements made in funeral orations in the past that have lived on in our literature. And I thought of other funerals I have attended or read about.

After the service for Brother Eyring, I said to his wife, Winifred, what I would have liked to have said to Henry. I told her that, in my opinion, his funeral service would rank in impressiveness next to that of Julius Caesar. Winifred said, "Henry would have liked you to say that." To me his funeral service, and many others I have attended, have furnished me with thrilling and exciting experiences.

I believe completely in the immortality of the personality, of possible eternal glory, of eternal progression and of the eternal existence of the human soul. I am confident that Henry Eyring will live forever in the glorious atmosphere of the celestial kingdom of God, which is the most stimulating thought of which I am capable.

I have also been impressed with the idea that Henry Eyring will live on in more ways than one, as will each of us. Henry was a teacher and a scientist. He started many people on a career of service. Our world will, from here on, be a better place because Henry Eyring lived.

In the science of crime detection, one fact accepted is that no person can pass through a room without leaving evidence of his having been there. It may be a footprint, a fallen hair, or a scent; and I am thrilled with the hundreds of evidences Henry Eyring left as he passed through this world. He made many changes in other people's lives as a result of his career of science, of his humanity, and of a faith which began in the Council of Heaven so many years ago.

In this I am reminded of the life story of Christopher Wren, the famous British architect, who lived from 1632 to 1723. He built many famous buildings in and around London, including the magnificent St. Paul's Cathedral. After his death, he was laid to rest in his cathedral masterpiece. On the plaque above his grave is this inscription:

> "Here is laid to rest the body of Sir Christopher Wren, the builder of the church and the city. If you seek his monument, look around you."

Henry Eyring left several monuments in the sons and daughters to whom he has given his genes, his personality, his faith, and his name. A person may live on in ideas in this world. Many men, women, and children die every year, yet some of them will live on in the memory and motivation of others long after their physical death.

As long as time lasts, George Washington will preside as the Father of his country in the hearts and minds of those who live in this free American land. Abraham Lincoln, whose mortal life was snuffed out by an assassin's bullet in 1865, is still a real presence throughout his country and the entire world. And he will continue to inspire many who are yet unborn.

Each of us is surrounded by a vast group of unseen friends who, though they are dead, yet shall they live. My parents still live on in my life. I still have a vital connection with my stake president, Henry H. Blood; with my high school principal, Leo J. Muir; my business tutor, Fred A. Wicket; my bishop, James E. Ellison; and many hundreds of other faithful friends and benefactors who still walk the paths running through my brain and heart.

With the hope of stimulating some important human values, I am devoting a part of this book to a few notable deaths and the various immortalities which have followed them.

Great Deaths

On November 22, 1963, the world was shocked by the news that John Fitzgerald Kennedy, President of the United States, had been shot to death.

At the time of the tragedy he and his wife, with a group of dignitaries, were riding through the streets of Dallas to address a meeting of citizens. He was smiling proudly as he accepted the admiring acclaim of his countrymen. Then in a moment he lay wounded and bleeding in the arms of his wife. Thirty minutes later he was pronounced dead.

This leader of the world's most powerful nation had been like a great oak upon the hill; and when he was cut down by the sniper's bullet, he left a lonesome place in our hearts, and gloom and despair were spread throughout the world.

Since that awful day, the life of John F. Kennedy has been memorialized in thousands of public gatherings and in the minds of millions. But in his death his influence has been much increased in our lives. His memory is now permanently enshrined in our hearts. In losing his life, it was made *greater*. Now we relive his childhood, we admire his devotion to his family, we honor him for his service in war, and we will forever be inspired by his friendly smile, his philosophy of service, and his whole-souled devotion.

In one of England's life-and-death battles with Napoleon, Horatio Nelson said to those under his command, "England expects this day every man to do his duty." It was this same spirit that actuated John F. Kennedy to say in his inaugural address, "Fellow Americans, ask not what your country can do for you, but rather ask what you can do for your country." By this philosophy he attempted to make our national strength superior to any enemy that might try to destroy it. It was in this spirit that he gave his life.

His body now rests in an honored grave in Arlington Cemetery, surrounded by other national heroes. Two of his children who preceded him in death are buried by his side; and we may well say of him as was said of the martyred Abraham Lincoln, "Now he belongs to the ages."

Above the graves of Gettysburg, President Lincoln led all Americans in expressing a high resolve that our honored dead shall not have died in vain. Rather, from their lives, we take increased devotion to bring about the birth in us of even greater things. The spirit of John F. Kennedy will join with our three other martyred presidents to enkindle an increasing national faith. And while we are horrified and ashamed that any human being would assume the ghastly responsibility for terminating any life, yet we know that the ideals and memory generated by the life of John F. Kennedy will go on forever.

The Apostle Paul said, "All things work together for the good of them that love God." That is, if we love God, if we think right, if we have the proper attitude and do the right things, then even this monumental tragedy will bring to all of us a blessing. Our lives are enriched and strengthened because of the law of opposites. Night is as necessary as day. Uphill is as beneficial as downhill. Labor is as important as ease. Sickness and death serve our eternal purposes quite as well as health and life.

If all of our prayers were answered, no one would ever get sick, no one would ever die. We would all get our own way and there would be no strength. Robert J. Ingersol once said, "If those we press and strain against our hearts could never die, perhaps that love would wither from the earth."

Like John F. Kennedy, President James A. Garfield was destroyed by an assassin's bullet. These men had much in common. Both were struck down in their youth. President Kennedy was 42 at the time of his death. President Garfield was 49. Both had young families; both were dedicated leaders; both had a love of the sea; both had a love of their fellowmen; and both were shot while on their way to address a meeting of their countrymen.

In one respect they were not alike. President Kennedy never regained consciousness after having been shot, whereas President Garfield suffered through a period of ten long, weary weeks between his injury and his death.

James G. Blaine, who served as Secretary of State under President Garfield, was chosen to give President Garfield's funeral oration, but it was much more than an oration. It was a gentle, tender, touching tribute to a friend, combined with profound and respectful admiration for a patriotic fellow citizen. Such a tribute further strengthens our resolve that the sacrifices of such men will not be in vain.

In part, Mr. Blaine said, "Surely, if happiness can ever come from the honors or triumphs of this world on that quiet July morning, James A. Garfield may well have been a happy man. No foreboding of evil haunted him; no slightest premonition of danger clouded his sky. His terrible fate was upon him in an instant. One moment he stood erect, strong, confident in the years stretching so peacefully before him; the next he lay wounded, bleeding, helpless, doomed to weary weeks of torture, to silence, and the grave.

"Great in life, he was surpassingly great in death. For no cause, in the very frenzy of wantonness and wickedness, by the red hand of murder, he was thrust from the full tide of this world's interests, from its hopes, its aspirations, its victories, into the visible presence of death; and he did not quail. Not alone for the one short moment in which stunned and dazed he could give up life, hardly aware of its relinquishment, but through days of deadly languor, through weeks of agony, that were not less agony because silently borne. With clear sight and calm courage he looked into his open grave.

"What blight and ruin met his anguished eyes, whose lips may tell. What brilliant broken plans. What baffled high ambition. What sundering of strong, warm, manhood's friendships. What bitter rending of sweet household ties. Behind him, a proud expectant nation; a great host of sustaining friends; a cherished and happy mother, wearing the full rich honors of her earthly toil and tears; the wife of his youth whose whole life lay in his; the little boys not yet emerged from childhood's day of frolic; the fair young daughter; the sturdy sons just springing into closest companionship, claiming every day, and every day rewarding a father's love and care; and in his own heart, the eager rejoicing power to meet all demands.

"Before him, desolation and darkness, and his soul was not shaken. His countrymen were thrilled with instant, profound, and universal sympathy. Though masterful in his mortal weakness, enshrined in the prayers of a world, yet all the love and all the sympathy could not share with him his suffering. He trod the wine press alone. With unfaltering front he faced death. With unfailing tenderness he took leave of life. Above the demoniac hiss of the assassin's bullet he heard the voice of God. And with supple resignation he bowed to the divine decree.

"As the end drew near, this early craving for the sea returned. The stately mansion of power had been to him a wearisome hospital of pain, and he begged to be taken from its prison walls, from its oppressive stifling air, from its homelessness and its hopelessness. Gently, silently, the love of a great people bore the pale sufferer to the longed-for healing of the sea, to live or die, as God should will, within sight of its heaving billows, and within sound of its manifold voices.

"With wan, fevered face, tenderly lifted to the cooling breeze, he looked wistfully upon the ocean's changing wonders; on its fair sails whitening in the morning light; on its restless waves rolling shoreward to break and die beneath the noonday sun; on the red clouds of evening arching low to the horizon; on the serene and shining pathway of the stars. Let us think that his dying eyes read a mystic meaning which only the rapt and parting soul may know. Let us believe that in the silence of the receding world he heard the great waves breaking on a further shore and felt already upon his wasted brow the breath of the eternal morning."

It has become a more or less common experience for many of this world's outstanding men and women, including many of the prophets, to give up their lives for what they believed. Our best information tells us that, with one exception, all the apostles of Jesus suffered violent deaths at the hands of others. There is something more than ordinarily impressive about sealing one's testimony with one's own blood. As the blood of the martyrs has always been the seed of the Church, so the blood of the patriots has provided the inspiration for our personal and national progress.

One of the most famous of all men was the ancient Greek philosopher, Socrates, who lived one of the most useful lives and died one of the most famous deaths of all times. And because his death helps us to better understand his life, we might profitably go back in imagination to attend the trial in 399 B.C. at which this wise man was condemned to die in the seventy-first year of his life.

Socrates, deeply attached to Athens, was a kind of self-appointed investigating committee of one to question what went on. He conceived it as his mission in life to help men see their own faults, to teach them the truth about themselves, and to try to get them to do what was right. Of course he knew what everyone knows—that most people would rather be damned by praise than saved by criticism.

Socrates was much loved by some, but he was feared and despised by others. Finally he was arrested and taken before a court of 500 citizen judges. His accusers charged that he taught false doctrines about religion and misled the youth.

In the trial, it was his privilege to speak in his own defense. Trying to help him, friends had prepared an address for Socrates to deliver to the judges. They felt certain that if this speech were to be read before the court it would be considered as an apology, and he would be freed.

But Socrates handed back the smoothly polished manuscript with a smile. It was unthinkable that he should now reverse his course and use his rich and powerful personality in pleading for his own life. Socrates reminded his friends of the years he had spent trying to teach people the difference between right and wrong. He could not now strike sail at the very height of his career.

Socrates made his own appeal to the court. It was an unusual discourse. Among other things he said, "Athenians, I am not going to argue for my own sake, but for yours. If you kill me, you may not easily find another like me, who, if I may use such a ludicrous figure of speech, am a sort of gadfly given to the state by God. The state is like a great and noble steed that is tardy in its motions. Owing to its very size, it requires someone to stir it into life. I am that gadfly which all day long and in all places am always fastening myself upon you, arousing and persuading and reproaching you."

Seeing that he was getting deeper into trouble, a friend said, "Socrates, why don't you hold your tongue? Then no one would interfere with you." Socrates said, "I may have difficulty in making you understand my answer. To hold my tongue would be disobedience to a divine command."

The greatest good is to converse about virtue and to examine oneself and others. That life which is unexamined is not worth living. Then Socrates recounted some of the evils of which his judges themselves were guilty. He said, "I have sought to persuade every man to seek virtue and wisdom before he looked to his private interests."

Socrates pointed out that while it is truly an evil thing to be full of faults, it is a still greater evil to be unwilling to recognize them. We do not wish others to deceive us; we must not deceive ourselves. He referred to the hypocrisy, pretense, and surrender frequently practiced by many in order that they might get along with people.

He said, "Often in battle one may escape death if he will throw away his arms and fall down upon his knees before his pursuers. If one is willing to say the things that are pleasing to his opponents, he may escape death; but the difficulty, my friends, is not in avoiding death, it is in avoiding ignorance and unrighteousness.

"Men in danger of death sometimes behave in the strangest manner. They seem to fancy that they are about to suffer some dreadful experience if they die, or that they could become immortal if they were freed. A good man ought not to calculate his chances of living or dying. He ought only to consider if he is doing right or doing wrong."

In referring to his own military service, he said:

"Strange indeed would have been my conduct, O men of Athens, if when I was ordered to attack the enemy at Anphipolis or Delium I had hesitated because I feared to face death. And what would be my present situation in believing as I do, that God orders me to fulfill a philosopher's mission, if I were to now desert my post through fear.

"Disobedience to a better, whether God or man, is evil and dishonorable. When God assigns me a task, sooner would I die a thousand deaths than to desert it. Men of Athens, I honor and love you, but I will obey God rather than you; and while I have strength, I shall never cease from the practice of teaching philosophy and exhorting all whom I meet of virtue."

When Socrates finished his statement, the vote of the judges was taken. Two hundred eighty voted for his death. Two hundred twenty voted for acquittal. Since he was condemned by a majority of thirty votes, the judges were required to sentence him. His fate was to die by drinking the juice of a poisonous herb called hemlock.

Even after his sentence, Socrates was given several chances to escape. The guards offered to leave his prison door unlocked if he would leave Athens, but Socrates rejected the idea. His life had been spent teaching people to obey law. It was unthinkable to him to repudiate his life's work by violating the law merely to save his life. He said, "I care not a straw for death; my only fear is of doing some unrighteous or unholy thing. I have never knowingly wronged another. Certainly I will not now wrong myself."

After the sentence had been passed, Socrates said, "Men of Athens, there are many reasons why I am not grieved at your vote of condemnation. It were far better to die than to live a slave." Then Socrates gave a long discourse about the reasons for his acceptance of the death sentence, and he reassured his listeners about death itself.

He said, "Therefore, I depart, condemned by you to suffer the penalty of villainy and wrong. I must abide by my sentence, you must abide by yours.

"And now, to you who have condemned me, I fain would prophesy, for I am about to die, and that is the hour at which men are gifted with prophetic power. I prophesy that immediately after my death a punishment far heavier than you have inflicted upon me will attend you. Me, you will kill, that you may not have to account for your lives, but you will have more severe accusers. If you think by killing me that you can avoid the just censure of evil, you are mistaken. Your only escape is to improve your own lives and make them more noble.

"Now to you who voted for my acquittal, the oracle that is within me tells me that what is about to happen to me is good, and that those who think that death is an evil are in error. Soon I will be able to converse with all the great and wise men of the past, and I shall be able to continue my search concerning truth and falsehood. Oh judges, be of good cheer about death, and know this of a truth, that no evil can ever happen to a good man, either in life or after death.

"I have but one favor to ask of you. When my young sons are grown up, I would ask you, oh my friends, that if they seem to care more about riches than about virtue, reprove them, as I have reproved you; and if they pretend to be something when they are really nothing, or if they care about those things for which they ought not to care, I would have you trouble them, as I have troubled you. If you do this, my sons and I will have received justice at your hands. The hour of departure has arrived. We go our separate ways, I to die, and you to live: which is better only God knows."

Socrates spent his last hours conversing about life's values. Speaking of that last discussion, one of his friends said that they felt like children being bereaved of a father. He said it seemed as though they must pass the rest of their lives as orphans.

Finally the sunset hour of execution drew near; the jailer entered and said, "Socrates, I know you to be the noblest, gentlest, and best of all men, and I am sure you will not be angry with me as the others condemned to die have been for I am not the guilty cause. You know my errand; therefore, will you try to bear lightly what must needs be." Then, bursting into tears, he left the room.

Turning to his friends, Socrates said, "How charming a man he is. While I have been in prison he has often come to visit me, and see now, how generously he sorrows. But we must do as he says—let the cup be brought."

Then a servant carrying the cup of poison entered the room. Holding it to his lips, quite cheerfully, Socrates drank the hemlock. His friend, Crito, said, "Such was the end of him, whom I may truly call the wisest and best man I have ever known."

Socrates was called a philosopher, which means a lover of wisdom. His death took place 2,365 years ago, and yet one of the collective needs of our individual lives, is for some wise person to serve us in the philosopher's office with emphasis upon its gadfly functions.

Everyone has a host of friends, but not many effective gadflies will be found among them. There are not many people like Socrates who love truth more than flattery, or wisdom or righteousness more than the good opinion of thoughtless friends. We need someone wise enough to know the truth and have the courage to sting us a bit when it is necessary.

Robert Burns said,

> O would some power the gift to gi'e us
> To see ourselves as others see us.
> It would from many a folly free us
> And foolish blunder save us.

Wouldn't it be stimulating if we could hear what our friends say and think about us behind our backs? Yet they are often willing to let us suffer the results of our mistakes because they lack the courage to tell us the truth. This fault is particularly noticeable as it applies to those who hold some station above us. There is an old saying that "everyone lies to the king." No one ever tells the king the truth; everyone tries to deceive the boss and those whose good will we most desire.

However, this thankless office of helping other people is where many of the world's most noble men and women have been called to serve. The people of his day wanted to destroy Socrates because he talked to people about their sins and tried to picture for them the problems that would arise in their lives if they didn't turn from their evil. Error is most uncomfortable in the presence of truth.

In the early 1940s, President Franklin D. Roosevelt wrote to Sir Winston Churchill. He said, "It is fun to live in the same decade with you." When we love some noble quality in another, we usually tend to embody it in ourselves.

I recently felt some similarly pleasing emotions as I read an account of the life of Joan of Arc. It was written by Louis de Conte, who was constantly by her side as her page and secretary during her long war. The account was published in two volumes by Mark Twain under the title of *Personal Recollections of Joan of Arc.*

Her biography itself is unique. It was written in court and comes to us under oath from the witness stand. It was taken from the official records of the great trial held in the year 1431, at which she was condemned to be burned alive. Every intimate detail of her short and eventful life is still preserved in the National Historical Archives of France.

Joan of Arc was born in the little village of Domremy, France, in 1412. Throughout her childhood, she was extraordinarily healthy and happy. She was wholehearted in her play. Her merry disposition was supplemented by a warm, sympathetic nature. She had frank, winning ways, was genuinely religious, and she was greatly admired and loved by everyone.

During this period in history, France was suffering cruel pains of its Hundred Years' War with England. France had lost almost every battle. Eight thousand Englishmen had wiped out sixty thousand Frenchmen at Agincourt. French courage had been paralyzed, and France had been reduced to little more than a British province. For Joan, who carried France upon her heart, the continual atrocities of war greatly sobered her spirit and frequently reduced her to tears. Then, in her thirteenth year, Joan began to hear voices, telling her that she would be God's instrument in setting France free.

Among her instructors were Saint Margaret and Saint Catherine. Three years were required to prepare her for her mission. At first she had offered objections. She said to her instructors, "But I am so young to leave my home and mother. How can I talk with men and be a comrade of soldiers? I am only a girl and know nothing of war or even how to ride a horse. How can I lead armies?" Her voice was often broken with sobs, but finally she accepted her call and said, "If it is commanded, I will go. I know that France will rise again, for God has ordained her to be free."

Her voices told her to go to the Governor of Vaucouleurs who would provide her with an escort of men-at-arms and send her to the Dauphin, who was the uncrowned heir to the throne. In leaving her village home, Joan said, "I am enlisted. God helping me, I will not turn back until the British grip is loosened from the throat of France." When the governor had heard her message he said, "What nonsense is this? You are but a child." But Joan said, "Nevertheless, I am appointed by the King of Heaven to lead the armies of France to raise the British siege of Orleans and crown the Dauphin at Rheims."

When the news reached the Dauphin that an unlearned seventeen-year-old peasant maid was coming to see him with a divine commission to free France, he appointed a committee of court advisors to hear her message. Confronting the committee she said, "Forgive me, reverend sirs, but I have no message save for the ears of his Grace, the Dauphin." Their arguments and threats were useless.

After they had left in great anger, she said to her friends, "My mission is to move the Dauphin by argument and reasoning to give me men-at-arms and send me to the siege. Even if the committee carried the message in the exact words with no word missing, and yet left out the persuasions of gesture, the supplicating tone and beseeching looks that form the words and make them live, then where were the value of that argument and whom could it convince?"

This untaught child had just discarded her shepherd's crook, and yet she was able to penetrate the cunning devices of trained men and defeat them at their own game. She would soon stand unafraid before nobles and other mighty men; she was fully prepared to clothe herself in steel and become the deliverer of France.

When she finally gained an audience with him, the Dauphin said to her, "Tell me who you are." Joan said, "I am called Joan the Maid. I am sent to say to you that the King of Heaven wills that you should give me men-at-arms and set me at my appointed work. For I will raise the siege of Orleans and break the British power." But how could she win victories for France where the nation's best-trained generals had had nothing but defeats for over fifty years? But Joan had said that "When God fights, it is a small matter whether the hand that holds the sword is big or little."

This unlearned girl said to the Dauphin, "Be not afraid. God has sent me to save you." Everyone knew that in her heart there was something that raised her above the greatest men of her day. Whether she came of God or not, they could feel that mysterious something that was later to put heart into her soldiers and turn mobs of cowards into armies of fighters. Her men forgot what fear was when they were in her presence. Her soldiers went into battle with joy in their eyes and a song on their lips. She swept over the battlefield like an irresistible storm. The Dauphin knew that was the only spirit which could save France, come from whence it may.

Joan won the confidence of the Dauphin and the court with her sweetness, simplicity, sincerity, and unconscious eloquence. The best and the most capable among them recognized that she was formed on a grander plan and moved on a loftier plane than the ordinary mass of mankind. And whence could come such sublime courage and conviction but from God himself?

Finally Joan was given her command. In a public proclamation the Dauphin said, "Know all men, that the most illustrious Charles, by the grace of God, King of France, is pleased to confer upon this well-beloved servant, Joan of Arc, called the Maid, the title, emoluments, and authorities of General-in-Chief of the armies of France."

A suit of armor was made for her at Tours. It was of the finest steel, heavily plated with silver, richly ornamented with the engraved designs and polished like a mirror. She was miraculously provided with a sacred sword long hidden behind the alter of St. Catherine's at Fierbois. She herself designed and consecrated a banner which she always carried with her into battle.

As the war march of Joan of Arc began, the curtain went up on one of the most unusual of all military careers. Louis Kossuth said that "Since the writing of human history began, Joan of Arc is the only person of either sex who has ever held supreme command of the military forces of a great nation at age seventeen." She rode a white horse and carried in her hand the sacred sword of Fierbois. It was also the symbol of her authority and the righteousness which she always maintained. She once said to her generals that even the "rude business of war could be better conducted without profanity or any of the other brutalities of speech."

Some could not understand why Joan continued to be alert, vigorous, and confident while her strongest men were exhausted by heavy marches and exposure. They might have reflected that a great soul with a great purpose can make a weak body strong and able to bear the most exhausting fatigues.

Once with an almost impossible objective ahead, Joan said to one of her generals, "I will lead the men over the wall." The general replied, "Not a man will follow you." Joan said, "I will not look back to see whether anyone is following or not."

But the soldiers of France did follow Joan of Arc. With her sacred sword, her consecrated banner, and her belief in her mission, she swept all before her. She sent a thrill of courage and enthusiasm through the French army such as neither king nor generals could produce. Then on May 8, 1430, by sheer strategy and force, she broke the siege at Orleans. This anniversary is still celebrated in France as "Joan of Arc Day." It is the day that she drove out the British and saved France. Then at the head of her troops she marched to Rheims and crowned the Dauphin king.

With her mission accomplished, Joan planned to return to her family in Domremy, but she was treacherously betrayed and sold to the British. Then her long trial of over a year began. For many weary months she was kept in chains. She was threatened and abused. Her judges and jurors were carefully selected enemies. Trumped-up charges of witchcraft and sorcery were brought against her. No one doubted that she had seen and conversed with supernatural beings. She had made many, many prophecies and had done many things that could not otherwise be explained.

But her enemies argued that her success came from Satan rather than from God; therefore, she must be destroyed. Church influence and civil power were both used to discredit her. She was promised her freedom if she would deny her voices and her mission. But Joan was immovable. She said, "If I were under sentence and saw the fire before me, or even if I were in flames themselves, I would not say other than what I have said at these trials, and I will abide by my testimony until I die."

A full year had now passed since she had gone speeding across the plain at the head of her troops, her silver helmet shining, her silvery cape fluttering in the wind, her white plumes flowing and her sword held aloft. But Joan of Arc would ride no more. And as the fires were being lighted around the stake at which this nineteen-year-old French peasant maid would be burned alive, she was again given a chance to regain her liberty by denying what she believed.

In choosing death's fire above her freedom, she said, "The world can use these words. I know this now—every man gives his life for what he believes; every woman gives her life for what she believes." People may believe in little or nothing, yet they give their lives to that little or nothing. "One life is all we have, and we live it as we believe in living it and then that life's gone. But to surrender what you are, and live without belief, is more terrible than dying, even more terrible than dying young."

Twenty-four years after her death, the Pope appointed a commission to examine the facts of Joan's life, and to award a judgment. The commission sat at Paris, at Domremy, at Rouen, and at Orleans. It worked for several months and reinvestigated every detail of her life. It examined the trial records and hundreds of personal witnesses. And through all of this exhaustive examination, Joan's character remained as spotless as it had always been.

As a result of the Pope's official investigation, Joan of Arc was canonized a saint. This praise was placed upon the official record of her life, there to remain forever.

It has been said that Joan of Arc lived in the most brutal and wicked time since the Dark Ages. But Joan was truthful when lying was the common speech of man. She was honest when honesty was a lost virtue. She maintained her personal dignity, unimpaired in an age of fawnings and servilities.

She had dauntless courage when hope had perished in the hearts of her countrymen. She was spotlessly pure in mind and body when most of society was foul in both. In her nineteen short years, this untaught girl had become the deliverer of France, the savior of her country. Hers was the genius of patriotism and embodiment of sainthood, with a martyr's crown upon her head. All of this Joan of Arc was when crime was the common business of mankind. These qualities developed by Joan of Arc may be continued forever in our lives.

Mohandas K. Gandhi, the patriot of India, was great in his life. But he was also great in his death. As the bullet of a crazed fanatic entered his scantily clad body, Gandhi raised his hands in prayer and used his last breath to bless his assassin.

Gandhi wore only the common dhoti. He lived in a mud hut that had no electric lights, running water, nor telephone. He didn't own an automobile, he never sought or even held a public office. He was without political post, academic distinction, scientific achievement, or artistic gift. He commanded no armies, led no diplomats, and owned no property; yet men with great governments and powerful armies behind them paid him homage.

The leaders of the British government soon discovered that England could not rule India against Gandhi and it could not rule India without Gandhi. By the sheer power of his personality, Gandhi raised himself to become the unquestioned leader of many millions of people, and he was as close to being India as anyone or anything could possibly be.

He was the most powerful man in his country. With united accord, Gandhi's followers renamed him, "The Mahatma," meaning "the great soul." And no title could have described him more appropriately.

Gandhi's life started out in a hole. He was burdened down with rather serious handicaps. He was afraid of the dark; he was afraid of people; he was afraid of himself; and he regarded himself as a coward. In addition, he had very damaging inferiority complexes. He had an uncontrollable temper and rather serious sex problems.

Realizing the disadvantages these traits gave him, Gandhi deliberately started out to remake himself, and some time before his death at age 78, he described himself as a "self re-made man." For anyone who is looking for a good phrase with startling possibilities, here is one of the best. No performance can be better than the person or the performer.

One of the greatest ambitions of Gandhi's life was to free his country. But he felt that, before he could free India from the British, he must free himself from those weaknesses which were holding him down. Gandhi determined to put himself under the perfect control of himself, because more than anything else he desired to be an effective instrument of negotiation for his country's welfare. How well he succeeded is known to everyone.

One of Gandhi's biographers stated that not since Socrates has the world seen Gandhi's equal for effective self-analysis with absolute composure and self-control. By some, he was thought to be the world's most Christ-like person, and yet he was not a Christian.

Gandhi believed in being, not merely in having or in seeming. He believed that the discord between deed and creed lay at the root of innumerable wrongs in his civilization; that was the major weakness of churches, states, parties, and persons. Gandhi thought that to believe a thing and not to practice it was dishonest, and that this gave institutions and men split personalities.

Gandhi never trifled; he never wavered; he never stumbled into success. He went on long fasts for discipline. He reasoned that if he could not curb his passion for food, how could he handle the more difficult situations in life itself? He said, "How can I control others if I cannot control myself?"

With Gandhi, to believe was to act. There was no pretense; face-saving was to him an unintelligible concept. Even while fighting for India's independence, Gandhi had the constant respect and trust of the British leaders. He had two mottos: "Harmony in adversity" and "Love despite differences."

There came a time during the bitter years of World War II when the fate of England hung in the balance. England could not spare even a single soldier to fight in defense of India. Many prominent Indian leaders were in favor of overthrowing the oppressive British rule while England was helpless, but Gandhi said no. He said, "We will not steal even our independence."

Gandhi's mother had taught him that eating meat was wrong, inasmuch as it necessitated the destruction of other life. And so young Gandhi made a pledge to his mother that he would remain a strict vegetarian throughout his life. Many years after Gandhi's mother had passed away, Gandhi himself became very ill. He was not expected to live. His physicians tried to persuade him that to drink a little beef broth might save his life, but Gandhi said, "Even for life itself we may not do certain things. There is only one course open to me—to die but never break my pledge."

Imagine what it would mean to our world if present-day leaders of nations had that kind of integrity. Then every man's word could be absolutely depended upon; trust, competence, and mutual respect would be the foundation of every human relationship and every national action. It was in these departments of personal greatness that Gandhi excelled. Everyone understood that Gandhi was absolutely honest; that he could be trusted; that his motives were right. When Gandhi said something, everyone knew that what he said was exactly what he meant. Millions trusted Gandhi; millions obeyed him; multitudes counted themselves as his followers; but strangely enough, only a few ever attempted to do as he did. Gandhi's greatness lay in doing what everyone could, but did not, do.

Then came that fateful day, July 30, 1948, at 5:05 p.m. Gandhi was hurrying to the village prayer ground. In the front row of the congregated worshipers sat one Nathuran Godse, who clutched a pistol in his pocket. As the two men almost touched each other, Godse fired three bullets into the body of the Mahatma. In response to Godse's obeisance, Gandhi touched his palms together, smiled, and blessed him.

Gandhi's mortal life came to an end. But even in the instant before death, this little brown man was engaged in the act of blessing people.

A few minutes after Gandhi's death, Prime Minister Nehru went on the radio. He said, "The light has gone out of our lives, and there is darkness everywhere, for our beloved leader, the father of our nation, is no more." At Godse's trial he said he bore no ill will to Gandhi. He said, "Before I fired the shots, I actually wished him well and bowed to him in reverence."

From this one example we might understand what power can be built into human lives. We need only to develop to their highest level God-given qualities with which each of us is endowed.

We speak often about the immortality of the soul as being our most important human concept, but even that would be relatively meaningless if it were not for the immortality of the personality. We would not like to resurrect an inferior body, but how would we like to resurrect an inferior personality?

So unlimited in its scope is personality that we even think of God himself in those terms. Perhaps our greatest single idea is that God is a real person. He is our Eternal Father. He is all-wise and all-knowing, and He has a personality developed to its maximum. The motives that lead men to seek God's guidance and blessings indicate His personality. That is, physical *things* do not forgive us, love us, nor work for our betterment and happiness.

A religious writer said, "There is a tendency to suppose that life everlasting simply means that our individual lives are merged like drops of rain and go back into the eternal ocean and are lost. If this were true, life itself would lose most of its meaning."

What a thrilling idea that in eternity every individual will be himself—a personal, separate, individual being, conscious of himself, conscious of others, and conscious of God. If it is true that most of our success, both here and hereafter, is based on our personality, then why shouldn't we spend more time thinking about getting our personality ready to support the weight of our eternal destiny?

Personality is the instrument we use in earning our daily bread. It is also the instrument of every other success, including that of attaining our eternal exaltation. By the effective use of our personality and character, we become like God. Our greatest opportunity is that we may build these traits in ourselves, based on those eternal principles that God himself has formulated for our benefit.

Another of history's most tragic deaths took place on June 27, 1844, when a mob with painted faces and murderous hearts gathered around the jail of Carthage, Illinois, where Joseph Smith, the prophet of the latter days, was imprisoned. Members of the mob, not content with the Prophet's unjust confinement, raided the jail. With one assassin's bullet they sent into eternity, at the age of 38, one of the greatest souls who has ever lived. Joseph Smith also sealed his testimony with his blood. And while his earthly remains have been consigned to fill another martyr's grave, his testimony lives on in the hearts of millions of people and is forever binding upon the world.

As we recall these many untimely deaths, we are lead inevitably to think of the greatest life which suffered the most tragic death of all. Next to the Father himself, the greatest intelligence of heaven came into the world to bring about our eternal exaltation. But at nine o'clock one Friday morning, He was hanged upon a cross on Mt. Calvary just outside the city of Jerusalem and left there until three o'clock in the afternoon. This crime was committed by the very people He came to save.

However, Jesus did not die. His life continues to bless us in many ways. And many other great men and women have followed that example. Some have given their lives for their country. Socrates gave his life for truth. Gandhi used his life to purchase the freedom of his countrymen. Joan of Arc gave her life to save France and was willing to suffer death for what she believed. Joseph Smith gave his life for his testimony of the gospel of Jesus Christ. Then above all these, with His life and death, the Son of God atoned for our sins; and on condition of our repentance He will redeem us all from eternal death.

Now our responsibility is to assure that our honored dead shall not have died in vain; rather, that their devotion and faith may continually stimulate greater life in us.

12

O My Father

Every human being has two creators; one is God, the other is himself. Without God we would be nothing. But even God cannot build greatness into us without intelligent, enthusiastic cooperation on our part.

The spirit of man, which came from our ante-mortal experience with God, is an architect which builds our body into its own likeness. A proper use of our fantastic mental endowment can make us anything we ourselves want to be.

William James, the renowned Harvard psychologist, once said, "How would you like to create your own mind?" But isn't that exactly what each of us does? In addition, we can also create our own bodies, our own enthusiasm.

Professor James reminds us that the mind, like the dyer's hand, is colored by what it holds. If I hold in my hand a sponge full of purple dye, my hand becomes purple. If I hold in my mind and heart ideas of enthusiasm, effectiveness, courage, and faith, my whole personality is colored accordingly. It is as true today as it was in Solomon's time that as a man thinketh in his heart, so is he in his life and in his accomplishment.

To help us in this projected enterprise of life, we ought to pick out several outstanding ideas and then, by habitual association and practice, we can make them a part of us. Thus we can form them into a philosophy which gives us the mental and spiritual power to determine the details of what we ourselves will sometime become.

A philosopher is a lover of wisdom, and a philosophy is a kind of wise mental code which we may think about and believe in and work at and fight for and live by. It also represents what we ourselves will become.

The Lord has told us to study the scriptures and to think great thoughts. If we read the Psalms and the Proverbs, we will understand much about the mind and soul building procedures of King David and his wise son, Solomon. We may develop the integrity of Job, the faith of the Apostle Paul, and the spirituality of Jesus of Nazareth. But, in addition, we can follow instructions given by the Lord to the people of our own day through Emma Smith.

The Lord himself suggested that the wife of the prophet select from the works of the poets and the musicians hymns which should be believed, memorized, and frequently run through their hearts. This would transform everyone who practiced them into a magnificent human being.

However, we frequently minimize the good results that may come from this philosophy because we let these ideas skate so lightly over our brain that they don't make much of an impression. Frequently we don't even remember them beyond the time spent reading them from the song book. For example, for over 65 years I have sung and loved Eliza R. Snow's poetical masterpiece, "O My Father." But I have followed the words from the hymn book or I have listened to the words of someone who sang next to me. When I couldn't remember one of the magnificent phrases, I would hum along on the tune while my tongue sang, "tra la la la la." But recently I needed to recall the words of "O My Father" without using a hymn book, and I discovered I was unable to do so.

Since then I have asked other people if they knew the words to "O My Father." In each case they have said they did. When circumstances permitted, I asked if they would actually demonstrate that ability to me. All these people have been good Church members, all have sung this hymn hundreds of times. Some have even been choir leaders whose business has been to direct the creative process of singing in other people. But I have yet to discover one who could recall the words without special rehearsal or prompting at some particular place. This means we may be using our hymn books as a crutch by which our spiritual power is being weakened.

Shocked by the embarrassment of this defect in my learning, I immediately went to work to memorize the words. Now I can get all of the one hundred eighty-four words which make up the four verses in exactly the right place without hesitation and without studied effort. I have now given myself the advantage of having transferred the spiritual wisdom of Eliza R. Snow from the hymn book to where it rests firmly in my mind and heart.

And I have been impressed again with the advantage great ideas give to our lives and our successes. I think about the life-saving scriptures, the inspiring philosophies, and the stimulating poems that may have rested so lightly in our minds that they have had little power over us.

It has been said that the poets stand next to prophets in their ability to uplift out lives. In some cases, poets may stand above the prophets in supplying us with a particular inspiration that will make us successful and happy. For example, I have never heard of Eliza R. Snow being sustained as a prophet, seer, and revelator, and yet she wrote "O My Father." I don't know of very many prophets as recorded in the holy scriptures who can make a more powerful thrill run up and down my spinal cord than does Eliza R. Snow's inspiration as contained in the ideas which make up the lyrics to "O My Father."

Suppose we analyze each verse of this hymn and make an appraisal of its value for our own success. Then we may proceed on a systematic basis to transfer the stimulating thrill and the constructive soul power from those words to us. Sister Snow wrote:

> O my Father, thou that dwellest
> In the high and glorious place,
> When shall I regain thy presence,
> And again behold thy face?
> In thy holy habitation,
> Did my spirit once reside?
> In my first primeval childhood,
> Was I nurtured near thy side?

The greatest fact in the universe is God. He is our eternal Heavenly Father. Our lives can best be studied in connection with His life, and they can best be motivated by getting His spirit into us. Our lives began with Him in that very important ante-mortal period where many of the most important values were established in us. In the first verse of "O My Father," we may actually relive our ante-mortal association with Him.

We worship Him for His greatness to us as we are nurtured by the presence of His spirit. We contemplate the necessary program by which we may regain His presence and again behold His face. We should frequently rethink these thoughts in our minds and hearts and recall the blessings of our first estate and our relationship with God. This involves all scriptures concerning "where we came from."

In the second verse, Sister Snow again leads us into scriptural truths which can generate pleasant meditations:

> For a wise and glorious purpose
> Thou hast placed me here on earth,
> And withheld the recollection
> Of my former friends and birth,
> Yet oft-times a secret something
> Whispered, "You're a stranger here;"
> And I felt that I had wandered
> From a more exalted sphere.

This verse involves us in that other important question of why we are here. It stimulates us to try to understand the purpose of our second estate and why God our eternal Heavenly Father made our birth "a sleep and a forgetting" (Wordsworth).

We sometimes get discouraged with our lives here, yet we are given power to solve our problems when we learn of that wise and glorious purpose for which our second estate was ordained, why the recollection of our first estate was withheld, and what our situation will be when that memory is restored. And while we are strangers upon this earth, we do come trailing clouds of glory from God who is our home.

Yet actually, in several ways, we are still strangers on this earth since our lives are based in heaven. We are here to be tested and proven and tried to see if we will do all things whatsoever the Lord our God shall command us.

Before we left our ante-mortal estate, we had come to a place where young people always come—where it is desirable for them to move away from the homes of their parents and to establish a home of their own where they may learn to stand on their own feet and do things—not because they are commanded, but because they are right. And, as offsprings of God, He has arranged that on our own power we may become as our eternal heavenly parents and return to our heavenly home after our mortality has been concluded.

As we think about God and heaven, as we sing this song, we might have the spirit of General MacArthur who said to the people of the Philippines, "I shall return." The program of MacArthur made it desirable for him to get back to the Philippines. But our assignment from God takes us back to heaven. And what an exciting idea that ought to be!

In the third verse, Sister Snow says:

> I had learned to call thee Father,
> Through thy Spirit from on high;
> But until the key of knowledge
> Was restored, I knew not why.
> In the heavens are parents single?
> No; the thought makes reason stare!
> Truth is reason, truth eternal
> Tells me I've a mother there.

What a tremendous thrill it is for a righteous soul to contemplate that heavenly home and the love of our eternal parents and each other.

If any "women's libber" would like to have something exciting to talk about, here is as good a place to begin as any. In the creation, God created men and women in His own image, "male and female created he them." And God blessed them and said unto them, ". . . Be fruitful and multiply and replenish the earth and subdue it." The sexes will be incomplete and unqualified for the highest degree of glory without each other and without the relationship which exists between them; a relationship God himself ordained and which we accepted in heaven.

In our ante-mortal existence we were each known by name and character. We fought the war in heaven under the direction of our elder brother, Jehovah, and our first earthly progenitor, who was previously known as Michael, the Archangel (or head angel). Then, as now, we were arrayed against the rebellion of Lucifer. What a thrilling thought it is that you will be yourself and I will be myself throughout eternity.

In the last verse, Sister Snow indicates important victories that may be brought about during this magnificent period of mortality, and implies an answer to the other important question of "where are we going after this life?"

> When I leave this frail existence,
> When I lay this mortal by,
> Father, Mother, may I meet you
> In your royal courts on high?
> Then, at length, when I've completed
> All you sent me forth to do,
> With your mutual approbation
> Let me come and dwell with you.

What a magnificent exercise it is to contemplate the highest kingdom, the heaven of heavens, and the blessings of being celestialized and looking forward to eternal life, eternal happiness, eternal progression, and eternal success with God.

Death is the event which brings about the most glorious eternal reunions. What a happy prospect. When our work here is finished, and with the mutual approbation of our eternal parents, we may return to live forever with God under the most favorable and happy of all conditions. This answers the great question asking, "where are we going after this life?"

If we sing Sister Snow's hymn merely for the music, we miss one of its most valuable advantages. And so occasionally we might repeat the lyrics aloud to ourselves as we feel the spirit of worship and accomplishment that goes with them, not for the music alone, but for the principles of truth and gospel meaning which lie behind the words.

And where is the scripture that could surpass, in religious content, the four verses of this magnificent hymn of thanksgiving, ambition, and worship? We ought not to miss, even for one time, the benefit of this inspiration because we don't know the words and must substitute "tra la la la la," instead of absorbing the feeling, the meaning, and the determination meant to be felt.

13

Thanatopsis

While William Cullen Bryant was still in his teens, he wrote a poem entitled "Thanatopsis." This word is made from Greek words meaning a view of death or a musing upon, or a meditation about death.

As a part of our meditation about death, we should also meditate about God. What a wonderful accomplishment to be able to say that we believe in God, that we believe He knows His business, that we trust Him, that He is all-powerful, and that He has our interests at heart. It would be difficult to imagine that death was merely some accident God could not handle or didn't understand.

We know that God can give life, and that He has power over death. God could banish death in an instant if He so desired. But nothing really dies at death. That is, nothing is really lost at death. This change was necessary and very desirable, even for the Son of God himself. If the Only Begotten Son of God voluntarily passed through the experience of death with the full approval and direction of His Father, then death is certainly a good thing for us also; and the most important part of our meditation is to make sure that we are prepared for death when it comes.

Mr. Bryant concludes his own meditation by saying:

> So live that when thy summons comes to join
> The innumerable caravan that moves
> To that mysterious realm where each shall take
> His chamber in the silent halls of death,
> Go thou not, like the quarry-slave at night,
> Scourged to his dungeon, but, sustained and soothed
> By an unfaltering trust, approach thy grave
> Like one who wraps the drapery of his couch
> About him, and lies down to pleasant dreams.

Just suppose that we could look beyond the boundaries of this life and see the beauty and wonder of celestial glory where God dwells. How difficult it might be to remain contented in our present situation. It would be a most dreadful misfortune if we could never die.

In the preexistence we walked by sight, we knew God. He is our Father. We lived with Him. But mortality is the period when we walk by faith. Terrible things sometimes happen to us when we fail to trust God.

A father who had not sufficiently meditated about death recently lost his daughter. When the little girl became ill, the father had hopes that she would recover. But she did not recover. At her death the father immediately became bitter and rebellious. He said that because God did not heal his child, he would not obey God.

He discarded his weak allegiance to Deity and discontinued all church activity. He began to drink and did other things he knew God would disapprove. Because of his conduct, he soon lost his employment. The mother was heartsick. The other children were confused. The family's happiness was destroyed and their eternal welfare was placed in serious jeopardy, all because this man did not understand and therefore assumed to judge God and to dictate to His will.

In a similar situation, someone asked, "What was God doing when my son died?" His friend replied, "He was probably doing the same thing He was doing when His own Son died." He was carrying out the divine plan made in our interest.

An unknown author has given us an interesting point of view about our relationship with God with the following story.

Footprints In The Sand

One night a man had a dream. He dreamed he was walking along the beach with the Lord. Across the sky flashed scenes from his life. For each scene, he noticed two sets of footprints in the sand: one belonging to him and the other to the Lord.

When the last scene flashed before him, he looked back at the footprints and noticed that many times along the path there was only one set of footprints in the sand. He also noticed that this happened during the lowest and saddest times in his life.

This really bothered him, so he questioned the Lord. "Lord, you said that once I decided to follow you, you would walk with me all the way, but I noticed that during the most troublesome times of my life, there was only one set of footprints. I don't understand why, when I needed you the most, you deserted me."

The Lord replied, "My precious, precious child. I love you and would never leave you. During your times of trial and suffering, when you see only one set of footprints, it was then that *I* carried you."

What a wonderful power in our lives some righteous meditations can be.

14

The State Of the Soul

Once each year, the President of the United States gives a talk before the Joint Sessions of Congress which is called "The State of the Union Address." In it he describes the progress made the previous year, the problems that need to be solved during the up-coming year, and what the plans are to solve them. This might be a good procedure to follow as we conduct our own affairs about life and death, because one's judgment is no better than his information.

On May 10, 1940, Winston Churchill was made Prime Minister of England. At that time, the mighty German Air Force was making round-the-clock trips across the English Channel, dumping plane load after plane load of bombs on England; and nobody knew whether the British would be able to hold on for another week or another month. Winston Churchill tells how he felt about his awesome responsibilities during those "darkest hours":

"As I went to bed at about three a.m. I was conscious of a profound feeling of relief. At last I had authority to give direction over this whole scene, and I felt as though I were walking with destiny, that my past life had been but a preparation for this hour, for this trial. I could not be reproached either for having made the war or for lack of preparation for it. And yet I felt I knew a good deal about it, and I was sure I would not fail."

What a thrilling thing it would be if we could get such confidence in our own human destiny so that we could predict where we will be and what we will be doing at a given time in the future.

Actually the Lord has given us much information about ourselves. He has told us about our ante-mortal existence. He has told us what the purpose of this life is. And He has given us alternate possibilities for eternity. He has told us how to qualify for each of the three degrees of glory, and He has also told us who will inhabit that area which is not a kingdom of glory.

We also have authoritative information about that intermediate state after the spirit leaves the body at death. And we also know much about what will happen when the spirit and the body are again reunited in the resurrection.

About this intermediate state, the Prophet Alma has said:

"Now, concerning the state of the soul between death and the resurrection—Behold, it has been made known unto my by an angel, that the spirits of all men, as soon as they are departed from this mortal body, yea, the spirits of all men, whether they be good or evil, are taken home to that God who gave them life.

"And then shall it come to pass, that the spirits of those who are righteous are received into a state of happiness, which is called paradise, a state of rest, a state of peace, where they shall rest from all their troubles and from all care, and sorrow.

"And then shall it come to pass, that the spirits of the wicked, yea, who are evil—for behold, they have no part nor portion of the Spirit of the Lord; for behold, they chose evil works rather than good; therefore the spirit of the devil did enter into them, and take possession of their house—and these shall be cast out into outer darkness; there shall be weeping, and wailing, and gnashing of teeth, and this because of their own iniquity, being led captive by the will of the devil.

"Now this is the state of the souls of the wicked, yea in darkness, and a state of awful, fearful looking for the fiery indignation of the wrath of God upon them; thus they remain in this state, as well as the righteous in paradise, until the time of their resurrection." (Alma 40:11-14.)

It is perfectly clear from many scriptures that this waiting period between the time of death and the time of resurrection is an inescapable necessity for the best interests of our lives. The scriptures indicate that man cannot be exalted in the flesh; that this separation of the body and the spirit is absolutely necessary so that the separation may be a fitting instrument of resurrection and exaltation. That is, a celestial spirit will be able to resurrect a celestial body. The quality of our resurrection shall be according to the glory by which our bodies are quickened.

It might be well for us to try to understand what it would be like to receive a fullness of the glory of God. Book of Mormon Prophet, Alma, uses the term "soul" as interchangeable with the spirit whereas another Book of Mormon Prophet, Nephi, makes plain that the spirit and the body are the soul of man.

"The soul shall be restored to the body, and the body to the soul; yea, and every limb and joint shall be restored to its body; yea, even a hair of the head shall not be lost; but all things shall be restored to their proper and perfect frame." (Alma 40:23.)

This same information is given in many places in the scriptures. In the gospel according to St. Luke, the Lord himself takes us behind the scenes into the spirit world. He tells us of two men. One He describes as a rich man. The other is Lazarus, a beggar, who had apparently lived a much better life than had the rich man. Both these men died, and the scripture says that Lazarus "was carried by the angels into Abraham's bosom: the rich man died also and was buried . . ." (Luke 16:22).

"And in hell he lift up his eyes, being in torments, and seeth Abraham afar off, and Lazarus in his bosom.

"And he cried and said, Father Abraham, have mercy on me, and send Lazarus, that he may dip the tip of his finger in water, and cool my tongue; for I am tormented in this flame.

"But Abraham said, Son, remember that thou in thy lifetime receivedst thy good things, and likewise Lazarus evil things: But now he is comforted, and thou are tormented.

"And beside all this, between us and you there is a great gulf fixed: so that they which would pass from hence to you cannot; neither can they pass to us, that would come from thence.

"Then he said, I pray theee therefore, father, that thou wouldest send him to my father's house:

"For I have five brethren; that he may testify unto them, lest they also come into this place of torment.

"Abraham saith unto him, They have Moses and the prophets; let them hear them.

"And he said, Nay, father Abraham: but if one went unto them from the dead, they will repent.

"And he said unto him, If they hear not Moses and the prophets, neither will they be persuaded, though one rose from the dead." (Luke 16:23-31.)

This tells us many things about the place in the spirit world to which we go. It also tells us something about the fact that, even without our bodies, we will be intelligent, recognizable individual beings with our own personalities, loves, attitudes, and memories.

Lazarus, the rich man, and Abraham all recognized each other. They could speak. They could be heard. They could see each other. They could understand each other. They remembered the details of their lives upon the earth, and they were possessed of the same emotions in the spirit world which had possessed them upon the earth. That is, after the rich man discovered that he could not improve his own situation, his next concern was for his family that still remained upon the earth, and he solicited help for them.

We will love there the same people we loved here, and we will be actuated by the same motives and ambitions. Even though the rich man was in this place of reformation, the welfare of his family was very important to him.

It is interesting to remember that even hell is a divine institution where those who have not been able to repent in this life will go to have their sins purged from them by suffering and repentance so that they will be eligible for the glory for which they could qualify.

After this important intermediate work has been done by God with our spirits, then will come that exciting event where each of us will be resurrected.

"The spirit and the body shall be reunited again in its perfect form; both limb and joint shall be restored to its proper frame, even as we now are at this time; and we shall be brought to stand before God, knowing even as we know now, and have a bright recollection of all our guilt.

"Now, this restoration shall come to all, both old and young, both bond and free, both male and female, both the wicked and the righteous; and even there shall not so much as a hair of their heads be lost; but every thing shall be restored to its perfect frame, as it is now, or in the body, and shall be brought and be arraigned before the bar of Christ the Son, and God the Father, and the Holy Spirit, which is one Eternal God, to be judged according to their works, whether they be good or whether they be evil." (Alma 11:43, 44.)

How grateful we will be then if we are worthy of resurrecting a celestial body.

If we know the laws and keep the commandments, we can govern our success and happiness in this life as well as during the interesting period when we are temporarily unembodied. Then follows that final period of eternal life when we may qualify for the celestial kingdom, which is the heaven of heavens. This is the headquarter's kingdom. This is where God and Christ are and where we may be worlds without end.

15

The Resurrection

Each Easter we rethink important thoughts having to do with our rescue from death and our resurrection from the grave. We remember the first glorious Easter sunrise which took place over nineteen hundred years ago when the glorious and universal resurrection was initiated upon this earth.

For more than one reason, Easter has been called the "Festival of the Dawn." It took place at the beginning of a new day, but it also signified some other new beginnings. Easter was a time when all nature was awakening in anticipation of the enjoyment of a new life. It also initiated the beginning of an eternal, everlasting existence for everyone who had ever lived, or who ever will live, upon this earth.

From the beginning, God has promised that every human being who has ever been, or who ever will be, born into the world will have a literal bodily resurrection. Some will come forth in the resurrection of the just and some will come forth in the resurrection of the unjust (Acts 24:15).

Our mortal spirits were added upon at birth with this wonderful body of flesh and bones for the temporary union we call mortality. At death that part of man which came from God lives on when that which came from the dust returns again to the dust. The prophets have declared that there must needs be a space of time allotted between the time of death and the time of resurrection for the cleansing of the spirit and the glorification of the body.

Because our resurrection is of such vital importance, we should always have facts concerning it clearly in mind. Because our judgment is no better than our information, it naturally follows that when we underestimate God, we shortchange ourselves. As our doubts and skepticisms increase, and as we half believe that God is dead or has lost His significance, we lose to that extent the power to give maximum uplift to our own lives. It is likely that our most important possible idea for Easter time, or for any other time, is that God lives, that Jesus Christ is the literal Son of God, and that the gospel message as recorded in the holy scriptures is true.

God still has the same almighty power by which the universe was created and is operated. He has the same omniscience that ordained the laws of the universe. He has the same ability to reveal Himself as He had when He talked with Moses face to face on the top of Mount Sinai. And yet, in our day of supposed intelligence and enlightenment, there are some who insist on depriving even God of His body, taking away His faculties and senses, and robbing Him of His personality. This is happening at the very time when He is preparing to come to the earth again with His holy angels in power and great glory to cleanse the earth of its sins and establish His own government upon it.

God has ordained our happiness to be the purpose of life. One of the primary conditions of happiness is to have a cleansed and purified spirit, inseparably joined together with a resurrected, glorified body. Occasionally we should go to a library, or the bookstore, and get some good books on physiology, sociology, psychology, personality, and religion, to help us try to understand what a tremendous investment God has made in our hands, our eyes, our brains, and our immortal spirits. God never does anything which is superfluous or whimsical.

The evidence of the resurrection is so overwhelming it seems incredible that anyone should fail to believe it wholeheartedly. Resurrection is reasonable, advantageous, scriptural, and a proven historical fact. Since time began, the promise of a resurrection has been continuously made through the prophets.

The most important death ever to take place upon this earth had Jesus of Nazareth as its principal. Many scholars believe that this death occurred at three o'clock Friday afternoon, some thirty-three years after His birth in Bethlehem of Judea, and three days before His resurrection.

The scriptures tell of the arrest of Jesus after dark on Thursday evening. All during the night He endured the mockery of a trial by being dragged before the magistrate of one political jurisdiction after another. Our present day runs from midnight to midnight. The Jewish day of this period went from sunrise to sunset, which might be from 6 a.m. to 6 p.m. The scriptures say, "And it was the third hour, and they crucified him" (Mark 15:25).

The third hour from six o'clock would mean that He was hung upon the cross at 9 a.m. on Friday. As He hung upon the cross, there were mighty disturbances in nature throughout the eastern and western continents. Mark says, "And when the sixth hour was come, there was darkness over the whole land until the ninth hour" (Mark 15:33).

The intensity of the disruptions in nature became the most intense between 12 p.m. and 3 p.m. The Jewish law made it unlawful for anyone to hang upon the cross during the Sabbath Day; and since the Sabbath began at sundown Friday afternoon, there was much concern that Jesus might not be dead before the necessary time. And so a number of the officials obtained permission from Pilate to break the legs of Jesus and His companions in death some time well ahead of sundown so that the increased agony would hasten their deaths.

But when, at approximately 3 p.m., they came to carry out this awful assignment, they found that Jesus was already dead. As the scripture records, at about the ninth hour Jesus said, ". . . My God, my God, why hast thou forsaken me?" (Mark 15:34).

"And Jesus cried with a loud voice, and gave up the ghost.

"And the veil of the temple was rent in twain from the top to the bottom.

"And when the centurion, which stood over against him, saw that he so cried out, and gave up the ghost, he said, Truly this man was the Son of God." (Mark 15:37-39.)

Jesus, the Son of God, had died. But on the third day after His death He rose. This central fact of our world history was actually initiated on the first Easter morning in the garden tomb of Joseph of Arimathaea on the outskirts of Jerusalem over nineteen hundred years ago. Matthew records this thrilling event as follows:

"In the end of the sabbath, as it began to dawn toward the first day of the week, came Mary Magdalene and the other Mary to see the sepulchre.

"And, behold, there was a great earthquake: for the angel of the Lord descended from heaven, and came and rolled back the stone from the door, and sat upon it.

"His countenance was like lightning, and his raiment white as snow."

"And for fear of him the keepers did shake, and became as dead men.

"And the angel answered and said unto the women, Fear not ye: for I know that ye seek Jesus, which was crucified.

"He is not here: for he is risen, as he said. Come, see the place where the Lord lay.

"And go quickly, and tell his disciples that he is risen from the dead; and, behold, he goeth before you into Galilee; there shall ye see him: lo, I have told you." (Matt. 28:1-7.)

Following this event, Christ personally ministered among the people as a resurrected being for forty days. He appeared to ten of His disciples in the little room in Jerusalem. However, Thomas was absent from this meeting; and when the disciples told him that they had seen the Lord, he did not believe them. Eight days later, Jesus appeared unto them again. This time Thomas was present and the Lord said to him, ". . .Reach hither thy finger, and behold my hands; and reach hither thy hand, and thrust it into my side: and be not faithless, but believing" (John 20:27).

After Thomas' declaration of complete conviction, Jesus said, "Thomas, because thou hast seen me, thou hast believed: blessed are they that have not seen, and yet have believed" (John 20:29).

Jesus manifested Himself again very early in the morning on the shores of the sea of Tiberius to many of His disciples who had spent the night fishing. Jesus stood on the shore, but the disciples knew not that it was Jesus. He said to them, ". . . Have ye any meat? They answered him, No.

"And he said unto them, Cast the net on the right side of the ship, and ye shall find." (John 21:5-6). They did as He said; and when they changed their nets to the other side of the ship, they caught many fish. And He ate with them.

Jesus had been seen and touched by many people on many occasions during this forty-day post-mortal period. Once He was seen by over five hundred brethren at once (see 1 Cor. 15:6). Then the record says, "And many other signs truly did Jesus in the presence of his disciples, which are not written in this book:

"But these are written, that ye might believe that Jesus is the Christ, the Son of God; and that believing ye might have life through his name." (John 20:30-31).

John the Revelator told us something about the resurrected Christ when he said, ". . . His countenance was as the sun (when it) shineth in (its) strength.

"And when I saw him, I fell at his feet as dead. And he laid his right hand upon me, saying unto me, Fear not; I am the first and the last.

"I am he that liveth, and was dead; and, behold, I am alive for evermore . . . ; and have the keys of hell and of death." (Rev. 1:16-18).

In addition to this, new information about the resurrection has come into the world in these latter days. Since His visit to Patmos, the resurrected Jesus has again been seen on several other occasions. Soon after His ascension into heaven, He made a visit to the people of ancient America who were then living in an advanced state of civilization. He organized His Church among them and taught them the principles of the gospel, of which we still find evidence of in the hieroglyphics and traditions of their American Indian descendants. As with Thomas, He showed these ancient Americans the wounds He had received on Calvary.

Centuries after the apostasy following His crucifixion, He came to the earth again in the early spring of 1820 to reestablish among men a belief in the God of Genesis, the God of Calvary, the God of John the Revelator, the God of the western continent, and the God of the latter days. While Joseph Smith was kneeling in the Sacred Grove, praying for wisdom to know which of the contending creeds was right, he had an experience which he partially describes as follows:

". . . I saw a pillar of light exactly over my head, above the brightness of the sun, which descended gradually until it fell upon me.

". . . When the light rested upon me I saw two Personages, whose brightness and glory defy all description, standing above me in the air. One

of them spake unto me, calling me by name and said, pointing to the other—
This is My Beloved Son. Hear Him!'' (Joseph Smith 1:16-17.)

On another occasion, the Prophet Joseph Smith and Oliver Cowdery
were praying in the Kirtland Temple on April 3, 1836. The Prophet says,
"The veil was taken from our minds, and the eyes of our understanding
were opened.

"We saw the Lord standing upon the breastwork of the pulpit, before
us; and under his feet was a paved work of pure gold, in color like amber."
(D&C 110:1-2.)

In our own day the Lord has officially opened the great and final
dispensation of His gospel to prepare the way for His glorious Second
Coming. Other resurrected beings have visited the earth, restoring their
various keys and authorities. The commemoration of Easter is for this
purpose—that in believing, we might have life through His name.

After the miracle at the wedding feast at Cana where Jesus changed
the water into wine, the guest said, ''. . . You have saved the best till the
last.'' God has also saved the best of life to the last. The faithful will find
that the best and the most of life lies beyond the boundaries of mortality.

Branch Ricky, the famous baseball manager, was once asked to describe his greatest day in baseball. He said, "I can't because I haven't had
it yet." Many of our most important days we haven't had yet either, since
they will come after death. That is, our resurrection day will be a great day,
the judgment day will be a great day, and every other day after death will
also be a great day.

Jerome B. Bell gives us the following:

> What is this mystery that men call death?
> My friend before me lies; in all save breath
> He seems the same as yesterday. His face
> So like to life, so calm, bears not a trace
> Of that great change which all of us so dread.
> I gaze on him and say: He is not dead,
> But sleeps; and soon he will arise and take
> Me by the hand. I know he will awake
> And smile on me as he did yesterday;
> And he will have some gentle word to say,
> Some kindly deed to do; for loving thought
> Was warp and woof of which his life was wrought.
> He is not dead. Such souls forever live
> In boundless measure of the love they give.

Jesus is as much alive now as He was that day in Jerusalem when He
showed himself to Thomas. Many wonderful Christian peoples of the world
say that they believe in the resurrection, but this belief is supported and

supplemented by many people presently living upon the earth who bear their solemn and reverent testimony that they *know* there will be a literal resurrection. I bear my own witness that again in our day the divine assurance has been given, that His promise of a glorious resurrection will be kept to all those who believe in Him and obey His commandments. I humbly pray that God will bless our lives and help us to look forward to this promised event in our own lives.

Many years ago, when I was a young man, I heard a dramatic reading entitled "The Guardsman" which impressed me very much because of its spirit. It is evident from the scriptures that the only mortals who actually saw the Lord come forth in His resurrected state were the Roman guards who had been placed at the tomb by Pilate to make sure that the body of Jesus was not interfered with.

Besides the guardsmen, the women came first to the tomb. They were confronted by the angel of the resurrection who said to the women, ". . . I know that ye seek Jesus, which was crucified. He is not here: for he is risen, as he said. Come, see the place where the Lord lay." (Matt. 28:5-6.)

The scriptures say that, when the guardsmen saw the angel of the resurrection, the soldiers "became as dead men" from fear. And in this dramatic reading the author, out of his reason and imagination, adds details which might have been evident to one who saw Jesus come forth from the tomb. I would like to repeat it here because of the motivation that might be furnished as Maximus tells his sweetheart his impressions and experiences at the resurrection:

The Guardsman

A Roman officer who guarded the tomb of the crucified Christ tells of the resurrection.

"My Silvia, 'Tis long since we have met, so kissed,
So held each other to heart!

I thought to greet thee as the conqueror comes,
Bearing the trophies of his prowess home, but
Jove has willed it should be otherwise.

Jove say I? Nay, some mightier, stronger God,
Who thus hath laid his heavy hand upon me; no
Victor, Silvia, but a conquered man—who seeks to
Hide his weakness in thy love.

How beautiful thou art! The years have brought
An added splendor to thy loveliness. With passion
Of dark eye and lip rose red, struggling between
Its dimple and its pride. Yet there is something
That glooms between thy love and mine;

Come, girdle me about with thy true arms, and
Pillow on thy breast this aching and bewildered
Head of mine;

Here, where the fountain glitters in the sun among
The saffron lillies and I will tell, if so that words
Will answer my desire, the shameful fate that
Has befallen me.

Down in Jerusalem they slew a man, or God—it may
Be that he was a God—those mad, wild Jews, whom
Pontius rules, thou knowest Pilate, Silvia,
A vain man, too weak to govern such a howling horde
As those same Jews.

This man they crucified. I knew naught of him,
Never heard his name until the day they dragged
Him to his death;

Then all tongues wagged about him and his deeds;
Some said he claimed to be their king, some that—
He had blasphemed their Deity. 'Twas certain
That he was poor and meanly born.

No warrior he, nor hero; and he taught doctrines
That surely would upset the world; so they killed
Him to be rid of him.

Wise, very wise, if he were only man, not quite so
Wise, if he were half a God!

I know that strange things happened when he died.
There was a darkness, and an agony, and some were
Vastly frightened—not so I.

What cared I if that mob of reeking Jews had
Brought a nameless curse upon their heads!
I had no part in their blood guiltiness.

At last, he died, and some few friends of his
Took him and laid him in a garden tomb. A watch
Was set about the sepulchre, lest these, his
Friends, should hide him and proclaim that he
Had risen as he had foretold.

Laugh not my Silvia, I laughed when I heard
The prophecy; I would I had not laughed.

I Maximus, was chosen for the guard with all my
Trusty fellows. Pilate knew I was a man who had
No foolish heart of softness—all unworthy of a man.

I was a soldier who had slain my foes; my eyes had
Looked upon a tortured slave as on a beetle crushed
Beneath my tread:

I gloried in the splendid strife of war, lusting
For conquest; I had won the praise of our stern
General on the scarlet field; red in my veins
The warrior passion ran—for I had sprung from
Heroes, Roman born!

That second night we watched before the tomb,
My men were merry; on the velvet turf, bestarred
With early blossoms of the spring; they diced
With jest and laughter.

All around the moonlight washed us like a silver
Lake, save where that silent sealed sepulchre
Was hung with shadow as a purple pall.

A faint wind stirred among the olive boughs,
Me thinks I hear the sighing of that wind in
All sounds since; it was so dumbly sad; but
As the night wore on it died away, and all
Was deadly stillness; Silvia, that stillness
Was most awful, as if some great heart had
Broken and so ceased to beat.

I thought of many things, but found no joy
In any thought, even the thought of thee. The
Moon waned in the west and sickly grew, her light
Sucked from her in the breaking dawn.

Never was dawn so welcome as that pale, faint
Glimmering in the cloudless brooding sky.

My Silvia, how may I tell thee what next came to
Pass? I have been mocked at, when I told the
Tale, for a crazed dreamer, punished by the Gods,
Because he slept on guard; but mock not thou, Silvia!
I could not bear it, if thy lips should mock
The vision dread, of that Judean morn.

Suddenly the pallid east was all aflame with
Radiance, that burst upon our eyes as from
The noonday sun, and then we saw two shapes, that
Were as the immortal Gods, standing before the
Tomb;

Around me fell my men as dead; but I though
Through my veins ran a cold tremor never known
Before, withstood the shock, and saw one
Shining shape roll back the stone.

The whole world seemed ablaze and through the
Garden came a mighty rushing wind, thundering a paean,
As a victory.

Then that dead man, came forth! O Silvia if
Thou could'st but the face of him have seen.

Never was such a conqueror. Yet no pride was
In it—naught but love and tenderness, such as
We Romans scoff at, and his eyes bespake him
Royal. O my Silvia, surely he was no Jew—but
Very God!

Then he looked full upon me. I had borne much
Staunchly but that look I could not bear! What
Man may front a God and live?

I fell prone as if stricken by a thunderbolt;
And though I died not; somewhat of me died that
Made me man.

When my long stupor passed, I was no longer Maximus,
I was a weakling with a piteous woman soul; all
Strength and pride, joy and ambition gone.

My Silvia, dare I tell thee what foul curse is mine
Because I looked upon a God?

I care no more for glory, all desire for honor
And for strife is gone from me, all eagerness for
War. I only care to help and save bruised beings
And to give some comfort to the weak and suffering.

I cannot even hate those Jews; my lips speak
Harshly of them, but within my heart, I only feel
Compassion; and I love all creatures, to the vilest
Of the slaves, who seem to me as brothers.

Silvia, scorn me not for this weakness; it will
Pass, surely 'twill pass in time and I shall be
Maximus, strong and valiant once again, forgetting
That slain God. And yet, and yet, he seemed like
One who could not be forgot.

16

The Old Rugged Cross

The Reverend George Bennard was a deeply religious man who lived when our Twentieth Century was just getting under way. As an officer of the Salvation Army, and later as an interdenominational evangelist, he participated in many religious meetings in Michigan and New York. As he went about trying to build up faith and spirituality in the lives of the people, he felt a strong desire to write a poem worthy of the religion of Christ, one that would fill an emotional need in the lives of the people.

In an extraordinary way, George Bennard felt the spirit of the great scriptural passage that says, "For God so loved the world, that he gave his only begotten Son, that whosoever believeth in him should not perish, but have everlasting life" (John 3:16). It was George Bennard's thought that these lines reminding us of the Redeemer's sacrifice served to sum up almost the entire enterprise of human salvation. It seemed to him that the cross on which Christ died might serve better than about anything else as a visible emblem of God's relationship with men.

Later on, in 1912, while working in Albion, Michigan, George Bennard wrote a poem. It was centered around the cross on which Christ completed His sacrifice. Appropriately enough, he entitled his poem, "The Old Rugged Cross."

After it was set to music, "The Old Rugged Cross" soon won popular acclaim and was sung everwhere. And since that time, many people have had great joy in the symbolism that Reverend Bennard pictured as they sang this familiar refrain:

> On a hill far away stood an old rugged cross,
> The emblem of suffering and shame;
> And I love that old cross where the dearest and best
> For the world of lost sinners was slain.

Oh, that old rugged cross, so despised by the world,
Has a wondrous attraction for me;
For the dear Lamb of God left His glory above,
To bear it to dark Calvary.

In the old rugged cross, stain'd with blood so divine
A wondrous beauty I see;
For t'was on that Old cross Jesus suffered and died,
To pardon and sanctify me.

To the old rugged cross I will ever be true,
Its shame and reproach gladly bear;
Then He'll call me someday to my home far away,
Where His glory forever I'll share.

Chorus

So I'll cherish the old rugged cross,
Till my trophies at last I lay down;
I will cling to the old rugged cross,
And exchange it some day for a crown.

It is an interesting fact that even before the Master's death, the term
cross was often used by Him as a symbol for man's loyalty to God. The
burden of carrying the cross was intended then, as now, as a test of the
devotion and righteousness of those who counted themselves as followers of
the Son of God. Jesus said to His disciples, "If any man will come after me,
let him deny himself, and take up his cross, and follow me" (Matt. 16:24).
By this picturesque statement, the Lord meant to convey a much more
important meaning than that His followers should merely acknowledge
His name.

The burden of the cross is represented by the more difficult and more
enduring *works* that give our faith its life. Contrary to what is believed by
some, Christianity is not just a set of ideas; it is a set of activities. It is not
just something to acknowledge or to think about, it is something to do
and to be.

To take up the cross of Christ, and to follow Him, not only means to
be informed about His program, but also to learn to do the things that He
has asked us to do. There are many people who honor God with their lips
and pay Him tribute when things are going well. He himself pointed out this
human weakness when He said, ". . . they draw near to me with their lips,
but their hearts are far from me, they teach for doctrines the commandments of men, having a form of godliness, but they deny the power thereof"
(Joseph Smith, *History of the Church,* Vol. 1, p. 19).

There were many who followed Jesus merely hoping to receive some
benefit from His miracles. As in the days of old, so there are many now
who would far rather eat of His loaves and fishes than to carry His cross.

Some nineteen hundred years ago, under the weight of the cross, Jesus stumbled blindly toward Calvary. He needed the assistance of a strong, vigorous person to help Him carry the load of the literal cross. Because no one volunteered, this duty was forced upon one Simon, the Syrenian (Matt. 27:32).

That this service to the Master was a thrilling opportunity Simon did not realize at the moment, yet this small amount of forced labor was the one thing for which Simon was remembered. This brief association and service evidently had other benefits, as the scripture later refers to Simon's two sons as the "chosen of the Lord."

This privilege of carrying the cross of Christ is also our greatest opportunity. Our best chance to be remembered will be because we have done some good in His name. This most marvelous of all calls is now before us. How fortunate we will be if we do not make Simon's mistake of reluctance. Jesus is still saying to us, "Take up your cross, follow me" (D&C 112:14).

In speaking to His followers, the Master used another interesting figure of speech when He said, "Take my yoke upon you" (Matt. 11:29). Apparently Jesus had spent a good deal of time in the carpenter shop, and He probably had made many yokes to fit the necks of oxen. The yoke was a device to enable them to increase the amount of the work that the oxen were capable of doing without hurting their necks.

To carry the cross seems like a little more serious kind of work than merely to wear a yoke. One who uses the yoke effectively may be a good worker, but to carry the cross is the job of a believer, a disciple, and a friend. Jesus spoke a great line that also applies to all of us in our day when He said, "He that taketh not his cross, and followeth after me, is not worthy of me" (Matt. 10:38).

Simon from Syrene carried the cross of Christ up to the top of Calvary. Like Simon, we are also strong and possess great power and influence. Just think what could be accomplished if, with one accord, all would set their hearts on doing the Lord's work. Even one man can, if he will, change the morale of a whole community.

The cross has a kind of universal acceptance as the symbol of Christianity. But it might also represent the two most important commandments. In its physical makeup, the cross has vertical as well as horizontal dimensions. These are the same two dimensions possessed by the gospel of Christ. In both the gospel and the cross, the vertical standards point from the earth upward toward God. Certainly this upright standard fittingly represents the first of the two greatest commandments as it constantly reminds us to do our duty to our Heavenly Father.

To complete the picture, the horizontal bar reaches out toward our fellow men in love and service and therefore fittingly represents the second of the two great commandments. The prophet has said that when we are in the service of our fellow men we are also in the service of God. Next to the follower's love of the Father is his love of his fellow men and his desire to be of service to them. What a thrilling thing it would be for us to whole-heartedly identify our lives with these two great objectives symbolically represented by the old rugged cross.

In his poem, George Bennard indicates how one might feel if he had a strong emotional attachment to this symbol and the things for which it stands. Actually most things are not important for themselves alone. Frequently they are even more important for what they stand for in our minds and what they get us to do. We have many great symbols by which we live, among which are a ring on the finger, a light in the window, and a flag in the sky. But the old rugged cross comes in a little different category. It might appropriately represent the most tremendous facts in the universe: that the Son of God gave His life for us, and it is by His stripes that we are healed.

The second part of our religion is one of love and activity that reaches out on its horizontal dimension of service to our fellow men. We must do something about this opportunity while it is still available.

In *Julius Caesar,* Shakespeare has Brutus say:

> There is a tide in the affairs of men
> Which, taken at the flood, leads on to fortune;
> Omitted, all the voyages of their life
> Is bound in shallows and in miseries.
> On such a full sea are we now afloat;
> And we must take the current when it serves,
> Or lose our ventures.

But in spite of all of the warnings, so many of our Christian enterprises are lost because of lethargy and procrastination in us. Members of one organization were recently shocked when their secretary read to them a list of forty-six resolutions they had passed during a certain year, resolutions on which no action had ever been taken. As followers of Christ, most of us also have a lot of unfilled resolutions. Nothing is ever settled merely by passing resolutions, however excellent they may be.

Our most important opportunity always will be found in the formula given by Jesus when He said we should deny ourselves, come take up the cross, and follow Him. This is the way we may establish in our lives those important traits that are recommended by the symbolism of the old rugged cross. May God help us to carry it nobly.

17

Our Several Immortalities

The most important objective of life is the immortality of the personality and the eternal glory of our souls. Every human being is the literal offspring of God, endowed with His attributes and heir to His eternal destiny.

1. But man may have several immortalities. The most important is a promise from God that if we keep His commandments, we may live forever with Him amid the unspeakable glory and happiness of the celestial kingdom.

2. Everyone, including Adam and Eve, may have a kind of immortality through their offspring to whom they give their genes, their name, their mentality, their appearance, and something of their personalities, possibilities, and abilities, to reproduce themselves in their children.

3. George Washington died in 1799, yet he lives on in the minds and hearts of millions of people. Abraham Lincoln was martyred in 1865, yet he is still a living presence on Capitol Hill in Washington, D.C. Each of us has hundreds of people such as our parents, our teachers, our heroes, and our family members, who, though they are dead, yet live on in our memory and the ambitions they inspire in our hearts.

4. Some years ago, Norman Vincent Peale published a book entitled *The Power of Positive Thinking,* and the book has sold millions of copies. This book is still being read by millions of people to whom Norman Vincent Peale will continue to live in motivating and directing their lives.

It has been written that "He has succeeded who, when he has gone, in the heart of another is still living on." All the outstanding prophets, poets, and playwrites live on in some way after their mortal death. Think of the service done by the Apostle Paul through the fourteen letters published in the New Testament, which have been read by millions of people throughout the world.

I have greatly loved the Prophet Job who is yet alive to me, as every morning when I open the holy scriptures this Prophet gives me a transfusion of his integrity as he says to me, ". . . while my breath is in me, and the spirit of God is in my nostrils;

"My lips shall not speak wickedness, nor my tongue utter deceit.

". . . till I die I will not remove mine integrity from me.

"My righteousness I hold fast and will not let it go: my heart shall not reproach me so long as I live." (Job 27:3-6.)

And inasmuch as I follow his spirit, the Prophet Job lives on in me.

The greatest gift of God to us is eternal life in His presence, but we can also develop our other immortalities to our hearts content.

18

The Celestial Kingdom

One of the most important accomplishments of this life is to learn to live the principles of the gospel. Dr. Henry C. Link once said that nothing puts so much order into life as to live by a set of sound principles. And the most sound principles ever discovered are the principles of the gospel of Jesus Christ. However, these are not intended merely to put order into our lives for here, they are to put exaltation and eternal happiness into our lives hereafter.

The Lord has established the celestial kingdom as the objective of every one of His children born into this life; and if we are familiar with what the celestial kingdom is and what it means to us, it might almost seem too good to be true. After studying the principles of the gospel, one young lady was supposed to have said through tears of joy, "It is so wonderful I just can't believe it." But think how she or any of us might feel if, at the end of this life, we are accounted worthy to live in the glory of the celestial kingdom with other celestial beings, including God himself.

We ought to thoroughly understand that all of the creations of God are wonderful and in our best interests. They are all profitable to us when we comply with them. Think how lavishly nature rewards us for things we do in a material way. If we plant a bushel of seed potatoes in good soil, nature will give us sixty bushels back as a reward. A single potato carried to England by Sir Walter Raleigh in the sixteenth century multiplied itself into food for millions.

One tomato seed can multiply itself a million times in a single year. Ten forests can come out of one acorn. I once talked with a friend who had just harvested fifty tons of onions; all from one little bag of onion seeds.

Now suppose we ask ourselves this question: Does it make good sense to suppose that the Lord will reward us more for planting potatoes and tomatoes and onions than He will for planting seeds of faith, success, and eternal life in the lives of His children? Or have you ever tried to figure how much it would be worth to live forever in the celestial kingdom?

It might help us to make an interesting comparison if we would get a quotation on what it would cost us to live in the best hotel that this world affords. Not only will the celestial kingdom be far more comfortable and more beautiful than the best hotel, but the people who go there will be more pleasant and more profitable to associate with.

We think we live on a good earth just as it is, but our earth now exists in its fallen or telestial state. However, we have been told that, during the millennium, the curse placed upon this earth at the fall will be removed, the earth will be renewed, and its paradisical glory will be restored as it was in Garden-of-Eden days. Then, after the millennium is over, our earth will again be raised in its status to become a celestial earth, and we may entitle ourselves to an inheritance upon it.

The Lord has said, "Nevertheless, he that endureth in faith and doeth my will, the same shall overcome, and shall receive an inheritance upon the earth when the day of transfiguration shall come" (D&C 63:20).

The Lord has given us much information about the celestial kingdom and about the condition of those who shall have earned the right to dwell upon it. In a very important revelation given in Kirtland, Ohio, on December 27, 1832, the Lord said in part as follows:

"Now, verily I say unto you, that through the redemption which is made for you is brought to pass the resurrection from the dead.

"And the spirit and the body are the soul of man.

"And the resurrection from the dead is the redemption of the soul.

"And the redemption of the soul is through him that quickeneth all things, in whose bosom it is decreed that the poor and the meek of the earth shall inherit it.

"Therefore, it must needs be sanctified from all unrighteousness, that it may be prepared for the celestial glory;

"For after it hath filled the measure of its creation, it shall be crowned with glory, even with the presence of God the Father;

"That bodies who are of the celestial kingdom may possess it forever and ever; for, for this intent was it made and created, and for this intent are they sanctified.

"And they who are not sanctified through the law which I have given unto you, even the law of Christ, must inherit another kingdom, even that of a terrestrial kingdom, or that of a telestial kingdom.

"For he who is not able to abide the law of a celestial kingdom cannot abide a celestial glory.

"And he who cannot abide the law of a terrestrial kingdom cannot abide a terrestrial glory.

"And he who cannot abide the law of a telestial kingdom cannot abide a telestial glory; therefore he is not meet for a kingdom of glory. Therefore he must abide a kingdom which is not a kingdom of glory.

"And again, verily I say unto you, the earth abideth the law of a celestial kingdom, for it filleth the measure of its creation, and transgresseth not the law—

"Wherefore, it shall be sanctified; yea, notwithstanding it shall die, it shall be quickened again, and shall abide the power by which it is quickened, and the righteous shall inherit it.

"For notwithstanding they die, they also shall rise again, a spiritual body.

"They who are of a celestial spirit shall receive the same body which was a natural body; even ye shall receive your bodies, and your glory shall be that glory by which your bodies are quickened.

"Ye who are quickened by a portion of the celestial glory shall then receive of the same, even a fulness. (D&C 88:14-29.)

If we would like a constructive assignment to give to our imagination, let us try to understand what it would be like to receive a fulness of the glory of God, what it would mean to be like Him, and to have everything He has. That is our possible destiny. Many years ago, President Charles W. Penrose made this statement about the celestial kingdom:

"The earth will die like its product, but it will be quickened again and resurrected to celestial glory. It has been born of the water and will also be born of the spirit, purified by fire from the corruption that once defiled it, developed into its perfections as one of the family of worlds fit for the Creator's presence, all its latent light awakened into scintillating action. It will move up into its place among the orbs governed by celestial time, shining like a sea of glass, mingled with fire, every tint and color of the heavenly bow radiates from its surface.

"The ransomed of the Lord will dwell upon it. The highest beings of the ancient orbs will visit it. The garden of God will again adorn it. The heavenly government will prevail in every part. Jesus will reign as its king. The river of life will flow from the regal throne. The tree of life whose leaves were for the healing of the nations will flourish upon the banks of the heavenly stream, and its golden fruit will be free for the white-robed throngs that they may eat and live forever. This perfected earth, with its saved inhabitants, will then be presented to the Eternal Father as the finished work of Christ." (See Rev. 4 & 22, & others.)

In order to quicken our imagination, suppose we try to fill in all the other details of accomplishment, joy, and happiness to be found in the celestial kingdom. And then to give the power of contrast to imagination, suppose that we ourselves don't make it.

In my own case, suppose my wife qualifies, my children go there, my neighbors and friends qualify for the celestial kingdom, but I must be cast out. I must go elsewhere and live forever under less favorable circumstances among a less pleasant group of people. Maybe you can think of something worse than that, but I do not know what it would be, since the most devastating of all emotions is the sense of being alone, of being unwanted, and of being unworthy. I might argue with myself and I might argue with my situation. I might say I was born on this earth, which gives me a right to live upon it eternally, provided I qualify. But because I was too busy, or because I could not overcome my bad habits, I must lose its benefits forever.

Orson Pratt said, "Who in looking upon the earth as it ascends in the scale of the universe, does not desire to keep pace with it, and when it shall be cleansed in its turn among the dazzling orbs of the blue vault of heaven shining forth in all of the splendor of celestial glory, he may find himself proportionately advancing in the scale of intellectual and moral excellence.

"Oh man, remember the future destiny and glory of the earth and secure thy everlasting inheritance upon the same, that when it shall be glorious thou shalt be glorious also."

This brings us back to the main function of our lives; to get rid of our sins and problems through the marvelous opportunity we have to cleanse ourselves. The dispensation of Jesus was opened by the proclamation of John the Baptist in which he said, "Repent ye, for the Kingdom of Heaven is at hand."

This same admonition has been given in our own day when the Lord himself has said, "Say nothing but repentance to this generation." We may not like to think about repentance because it reminds us of things that are unpleasant, and we usually don't like to think about unpleasant things. Yet repentance may be the most pleasant, most exciting thing we can conceive of.

Some time ago, on one hot August afternoon, I found myself in southern Illinois in what was the most unpleasant weather I had ever experienced. The heat was intense, the humidity was high, and I was sweaty and sticky and dirty. But after the day's work was done, I was taken to an air-conditioned hotel where a reservation had been made. I took a hot, soapy bath and put on fresh, clean clothing. A little later I got into a bed between cool, clean, white sheets. Before dropping off to sleep, I lay there for a while and thought about repentance. I thought if it was this pleasant to cleanse the body of a little sticky perspiration, what might it be like to cleanse the mind and soul of guilt and to stand clean and pure before God. What a thrilling experience that would be.

Many years ago, John Gillespie Magee was an American fighter pilot flying with the Royal Canadian Air Force. He was shot down over London in the Battle for Britain in the first part of the Second World War. Before going into the service, John Gillespie Magee had done the usual things seventeen-year-old boys do; and, after his basic training was completed, he felt in his hand for the first time the controls of powerful engines capable of sending his aircraft through space at tremendous speeds.

Six months before his death, feeling an exhilaration that came from doing well his part of the work of the world, John Gillespie Magee wrote his memorable poem entitled "High Flight," now found in the Library of Congress under the title "Poems of Faith and Freedom:"

> Oh! I have slipped the surly bonds of earth
> And danced the skies on laughter-silvered wings;
> Sunward I've climbed, and joined the tumbling mirth
> Of sun-split clouds—and done a hundred things
> You have not dreamed of—wheeled and soared and swung
> High in the sunlit silence, hov'ring there.
> I've chased the shouting wind along, and flung
> My eager craft through footless halls of air.
>
> Up, Up the long, delirous, burning blue
> I've topped the wind-swept heights with easy grace
> Where never lark, nor even eagle flew—
> And, while with silent lifting mind I've trod
> The high untrespassed sanctity of space,
> Put out my hand and touched the face of God.

I quote these lines because each of us is also engaged in a high flight. We are engaged in the greatest high flight ever known in the world. We are on our way to the celestial kingdom. And may God help us to be successful in the accomplishment of this objective.

19

A Revelation Of the Celestial Kingdom

The Holy Bible, one of the most important resources of our world, begins its narration to us by saying, "In the beginning God created the heaven and the earth" (Gen. 1:1).

As the vast drama of earth's progress began to unfold, God created man in His own image. In the image of God created he him; male and female created He them. He organized His church upon the earth and announced the decree that everyone should be judged according to his works. He ordained that, under certain conditions, the offspring of God should become like their eternal Heavenly parents and live with them in God's highest order, which is known as the celestial kingdom.

Then on January 21, 1836, in the Kirtland Temple, the Lord gave a magnificent revelation to the Prophet Joseph Smith about this condition which should be prepared for those children of God's who had been formed in His image and should qualify for His highest place of merit during their probationary state of mortality. This vision is now recorded as the 137th section of the Doctrine and Covenants.

"The heavens were opened upon us, and I beheld the celestial kingdom of God, and the glory thereof, whether in the body or out I cannot tell.

"I saw the transcendent beauty of the gate through which the heirs of that kingdom will enter, which was like unto circling flames of fire;

"Also the blazing throne of God, whereon was seated the Father and the Son.

"I saw the beautiful streets of that kingdom, which had the appearance of being paved with gold.

"I saw Father Adam and Abraham; and my father and my mother; my brother Alvin, that has long since slept;

"And marveled how it was that he had obtained an inheritance in that kingdom, seeing that he had departed this life before the Lord had set his hand to gether Israel the second time, and had not been baptized for the remission of sins.

"Thus came the voice of the Lord unto me, saying: All who have died without a knowledge of this gospel, who would have received it if they had been permitted to tarry, shall be heirs of the celestial kingdom of God;

"Also all that shall die henceforth without a knowledge of it, who would have received it with all their hearts, shall be heirs of that kingdom;

"For I, the Lord, will judge all men according to their works, according to the desire of their hearts.

"And I also beheld that all children who die before they arrive at the years of accountability are saved in the celestial kingdom of heaven."

20

A Philosophy Of Life

The most valuable resource in the universe is life. That primal, mysterious element in which all of us, including God, has his being. The most important responsibility ever laid upon the shoulders of any human being is to make the best and the most of his own life. We need to know as much as we can about what life is and how it may be improved.

Shakespeare's Macbeth was showing little knowledge of his subject when he said, "Life is a tale told by an idiot full of sound and fury, signifying nothing." That is, to Macbeth, life didn't seem very important. Hamlet was also falling down badly when he said, "How weary, stale, flat, and unprofitable seem to me all the uses of this world. 'Tis like an unweeded garden that goes to seed. Things rank and gross in nature possess it merely."

Whoever was responsible for these expressions had not concerned himself much about the past or the future, nor had he taken much thought about what could be done in the present. So it is that life doesn't make sense for one who looks at it from a too limited perspective. Nor do we get out of it what was intended when we look at life through veils of ignorance.

The big three among all the questions of life are "whence," "why," and "whither." The Persian philosopher, Omar Khayyam, was a very wise man; and yet, at the end of his life, he confessed that he was no nearer to understanding life than he had been at the beginning. He said that he was going out the same door of life by which he had come in:

> I came like water and like the wind I go
> Into this universe and why, not knowing,
> Nor whence, like water willy-nilly flowing,
> And out of it like wind along the waste,
> I know not whither willy-nilly blowing.
>
> Up from earth's center, through the seventh gate
> I rose, and on the throne of Saturn sate,
> And many a knot unravelled by the way
> But not the master knot of human fate.

There was one door to which I found no key.
There was one veil through which I might not see.

We need more accurate, authoritative sources for our information about life and how to employ helpful motivations that will get us most effectively to our destination. I have great authority over my finger. If I tell it to bend, it bends; if I tell it to unbend, it unbends. If I tell my eyes to close, they close. If I give my feet an order, they obey. When I can get that kind of control over my brain and my tongue and my ambition and my enthusiasm, then maximum success is placed within my easy reach.

God has indicated that we are on a program of eternal progression which will lead to eternal success, eternal glory, and eternal joy. He had this ultimate objective in mind when He said, "Be ye therefore perfect even as your Father in Heaven is perfect" (Matt. 5:48). Another scripture points out that ". . . Men are that they might have joy" (2 Nephi 2:25).

To reach the ultimate objective, we need to have a strong philosophy about success. The dictionary describes philosophy as the science that investigates the most general facts and principles of reality, including those involved in our human nature and conduct. An effective philosophy of life would include one's religion. Therefore, a man's philosophy of life may be the most important thing he has. Most of our religious philosophy is centered in an effective program for our own exaltation and concerns primarily the preparation we make for our future.

We knew before we came to earth that we were coming to a place where there would be weakness and difficulty and sin to overcome. The Lord has said, ". . .They who keep their first estate shall be added upon; and they who keep not their first estate shall not have glory in the same kingdom with those who keep their first estate; and they who keep their second estate shall have glory added upon their heads for ever and ever" (Abraham 3:26). Maybe someone can think of a concept more exciting, but I don't know what it would be.

As birth describes the passage from the first to our second estate, so death describes the passage from the second to our final estate. Even the Son of God was once as we now are. Just before going to the cross, He mentioned both His birth and His death to His Heavenly Father.

"I have glorified thee on the earth: I have finished the work which thou gavest me to do.

"And now, O Father, glorify thou me with thine own self with the glory which I had with thee before the world was." (John 17:4-5.)

So it has been with Him. So it will be with us if we can achieve a sufficiently effective philosophy of life.

If one should err in believing the gospel of Jesus Christ to be true, one could not possibly be the loser by the mistake. But how irreparable would be the loss for one who should err in supposing the gospel of Jesus Christ to be false.

Suppose that there is a Christ, but that I should be Christ-less; suppose there is a Heavenly Father's love, but that I should remain an alien; suppose there is a heaven, but that I should be cast down to hell.

In 1852, John Ruskin entered a noble statement into his diary when he wrote, "Today I promised God that I would conduct my life as though I believed every principle of the gospel to be true." That is as safe and profitable philosophy of life as anyone could adopt. It does not seem impressive to me when someone is faithful only when he has an absolute knowledge of every truth.

But how inspiring it can be when one can be honest, righteous, and faithful on his own power, not only because he obeys God, but because he also agrees with Him. Certainly every thoughtful, intelligent man could tell that the gospel of Jesus Christ is the most profitable, successful, manly, happy way to live.

> Fired at first sight with what the muse imparts
> In fearless youth we tempt the heights of arts.
> While from the bounded level of our mind
> Short views we take nor see the lengths behind.
> But more advanced, behold, with strange surprise,
> New distant scenes of endless science rise.
> So pleased at first the towering Alps we try,
> Mount o'er the vales and seem to tread the sky.
> The eternal snows appear already passed,
> And the first cloud and mountains seem the last.
> But those attained, we trembling to survey
> The growing labors of the lengthened way.
> The increasing prospect tires our wandering eyes.
> Hills peep o'er hills, and Alps on Alps arise.

Alexander Pope

21

Going Home

One thing we can do to help us understand procedures better is to make more effective use of comparisons and analogies. When we compare a procedure we want to understand with one we already comprehend, then a new meaning becomes easier to acquire.

Jesus used this procedure in His famous parables. He also used the procedure to make His own calling more understandable to people. On one occasion He referred to Himself as "The Door of the Sheepfold." On another occasion He called Himself the "Pruner of the Vineyard." He also gave an interesting picture of Himself when He said He was ". . . the bright and morning star" (Rev. 22:16)—the morning star which heralds the approach of day.

He made interesting comparisons in honoring some of His children. He said, "Ye are the salt of the earth." He also said, "Ye are the light of the world."

We make similar comparisons for our own comfort and encouragement. As life gets nearer the end, we may say we are "going home." We are justified in making this reference, because of scriptural accounts that tell us we lived with God in a marvelous world of spirits and that at death the body returns to the earth as it was while the spirit returns to God who gave it.

In 1822, John Howard Payne wrote his musical masterpiece entitled "Home Sweet Home." At that time, Mr. Payne was living in Paris, far away from the old homestead he knew and loved so well. But John Howard Payne was going home. Home is where Mother and Father are. Home is where we grew up, and John Howard Payne was going home.

When death comes we go home. We go back to God. We go back to where our parents are and where many of our friends are. And if we do well, then we might sing with John Howard Payne, "There's no place like home."

May God help us to have a happy homecoming as we finish the tremendous experience which is our second estate.

22

To See God

Some time ago a group of college students was making a tour of the Church Office Building in Salt Lake City. I was asked to talk to them about the building and answer any questions they might care to ask. Near the end of the tour, one young woman raised her hand and asked, "Brother Sill, have you ever seen God?"

I was a little startled and felt I was not quite prepared to do justice to the question. So I said to her, "If you would permit me, I would like to give you three answers to that question. The first answer, in the spirit of what I am sure you had in mind, is no. I have not seen God.

"But that is not a completely accurate answer and requires an explanation. What I mean is, I have not seen Him since my mortal birth on March 31, 1903. But I saw Him a great many times before that time."

Nothing is more plainly written in the scriptures than the fact that the life of Christ did not begin at His birth in the manger at Bethlehem, nor did it end at His death on Calvary's Hill. It is just as certain that our lives did not begin when we were born, neither will they end when we die.

As the poet Wordsworth says:

> Our birth is but a sleep and a forgetting.
> The soul that rises with us
> Our life's star hath had elsewhere its setting
> And cometh from afar,
> Not in entire forgetfulness,
> Not in utter nakedness
> But trailing clouds of glory do we come
> From God who is our home.

There are many situations where all of the facts do not appear on the surface. For example, a strange sight is often seen at sea where the wind is blowing the water and surface ice all in one direction and then we see a great iceberg sailing in the opposite direction directly into the face of the wind.

What we need to know about this seeming contradiction is that down in the depths of the sea the iceberg is being controlled by powerful ocean currents that disregard the comparatively puny winds that control the surface ice and water. Therefore, my second answer would be that I have seen God many times before 1903. Since my mortal birth I have not even seen my own spirit and yet I know that I have one.

Answer number three is that while I have not seen Him since my birth into this life I know a great deal about him. I know what He looks like. I know what He wants me to do. I have read the testimony of a great many people who have seen Him during their mortality:

1. Moses spent forty days and forty nights with God on Mt. Sinai and talked with Him as one man speaketh unto his friend. Moses discusses God in such terms as, "his hands and his eyes and his voice."

2. I have read the description of John the Revelator when the Lord appeared to him on the Isle of Patmos some sixty years after His resurrection. I have read the description his disciple, Thomas, who was permitted to handle the resurrected Jesus and put his finger into the nail holes in His hands and thrust his hand into His side. I have also read a complete description of Him given by Joseph Smith, to whom God the Father and His Son, Jesus Christ, appeared in the sacred grove in New York state in the early spring of 1820. And again the resurrected Jesus appeared in the Kirtland Temple to Joseph Smith and Oliver Cowdery on April 3, 1836, as recorded in Section 110 of the Doctrine and Covenants. If you would like to have a thrilling experience next to seeing the Lord yourself, read the account given by one who saw and conversed with Him as Moses did face to face.

And there are many other accounts written down for our benefit by people who have seen Him since His resurrection on that first Easter morning.

The Lord has also promised each of us that we will see Him again many, many times. He has promised, "Blessed are the pure in heart: for they shall see God" (Matt. 5:8). He has also promised that He will soon come again to cleanse the earth and reign here during the millennium of a thousand years and all of us who are worthy may see Him.

After the millennium reign is over our earth will be raised in its status to become a celestial orb and the home of those upon this earth who qualify for the celestial kingdom. What a thrill to know in this adventure of life that God is our Eternal Heavenly Father, that for long ages we lived with Him and we may each look forward to a glorious period in His presence in the celestial kingdom.

23

My Father's Business

It is a very interesting thought that the Church is a divine institution. Some nineteen hundred years ago the Son of God was sent on an official mission to this earth to organize His church. His church was to be called by His name. Everything that was done in His church was to be done in His name.

The program of the atonement has been made known to us during this life that we might take full advantage of it. It was made known to us that the Savior would take upon Himself our sins on condition of our repentance and obedience to the requirements of exaltation.

During this life, we are supposed to learn about the importance of the family organization and about the eternal marriage covenant. It is important that we understand the literal bodily resurrection, eternal progression, and many other important concepts which are necessary for our eternal welfare and happiness. The Lord placed, in the Church, necessary officers authorized to perform these saving ordinances.

The contemplated plan was that man himself should have the priesthood conferred upon him by one having the necessary authority. He must repent of his sins and be baptized by water and receive the gift of the Holy Ghost. If it were not for knowing the facts and what the requirements are for exaltation, confusion would be everywhere. Holy temples must be built and saving ordinances must be performed therein where earth's families may be sealed together for time and eternity.

One of the major problems we have in life, however, is that the people for whom this program was given will not believe the word of the Lord. Because of this attitude, many people become criminals and sinners with a way of life which allows them to lie, to steal, and to cheat. In fact, to disbelieve the word of the Lord and to disobey His commandments seem to be two of the most popular activities of our day.

In addition to the Church being a divine institution, the Lord has said that governments were also instituted by Him for the benefit of man, and that He will hold us responsible for our acts in relationship thereto. Even though He raised up wise men to establish the constitution of our land, we continue to fight against it and to try to overthrow the government. Politicians do many things to get into office instead of trying to run a government which would please the intelligence of God, who is all-wise and who is working in our interests.

Our occupations were also ordained by Him. When He covered the earth with topsoil, He was looking forward to our agricultural and horticultural industries. He established the livestock business. When He taught Adam and Eve how to make coats out of skins, He began the tailoring trade. As He loaded our earth with minerals, metals, and oils, He was laying the foundation for our manufacturing, mining and transportation industries. He also established many trades and businesses.

Medicine is a process by which we keep ourselves well physically. Psychology, psychiatry and other studies of the mind are how we keep ourselves well mentally. Sociology teaches us to live agreeably together. Law keeps our lives orderly. In business we learn to deal profitably and agreeably with each other.

Elbert Hubbard said that business is the process of ministering to human needs. Therefore, said he, business is essentially a divine calling. A farmer who grows our food is ministering to human needs. Therefore, he is entitled to say he is engaged in a divine occupation. A doctor who once gave me nine blood transfusions was ministering to a human need, which also entitled him to say he is engaged in a godly business.

God has given us the science of religion to teach us how to keep ourselves well spiritually. Jesus himself made a reference to an enterprise He called, "My Father's business." Anything which is eternally helpful to us is included in our Father's business. He has invited us to join Him in this family enterprise, so that it now becomes our work to build character, faith, integrity, and a knowledge of eternal life into the lives of His children.

A man was talking with a friend who claimed to have a belief in God, and yet he denied belief in those concepts which God himself has ordained. He did not believe in a literal bodily resurrection. He did not believe that a literal family relationship existed beyond the grave. He believed that the death of the body ended forever all there was of human life and personality.

His friend said to him, "What kind of business do you think God is engaged in anyway? Do you think an all-wise and all-kind and all-good and everlasting eternal Heavenly Father would bring human souls into being, endow them with magnificent minds, inspire them to think the loftiest of thoughts, give them hearts to love with, endow them with hands that can work miracles, and then after a few short years completely wash them out as if they were of no value whatever?"

Reason itself should teach us that the miraculous creations of God are never lost. God himself is eternal and will live forever. Our most learned scientists talk of time in terms of billions of light years. What possible satisfaction could it be to such a God to allow His masterpiece of creation, represented by His Only Begotton Son in the flesh, to be wasted and lost after only a few short years made up primarily of childhood?

We can have no greater assurance of immortality for the offspring of God than that the parents themselves are immortal. An all-wise Creator would not perfect His masterpiece of human life in His own image, and when it had just begun to live throw it utterly away. What would you think of a businessman who would work intelligently and hard to get a business going, employing the best planning and the wisest use of resources each step of the way, and then wash it out every few months to begin over again?

Who could argue that the God who on four occasions said, "This is my Beloved Son in whom I am well pleased," (see Matt. 3:17, 17:5; Joseph Smith 2:17; 3 Nephi 11:7), would lose interest in Him, beyond the few years of mortality, the greatest intelligence of heaven next to God himself, after only thirty-three short years? Everybody knows that this body of flesh is temporary and for a good reason. God himself has said that we should live on eternally.

One of the most important convictions of our lives should be that our Father's business, of building up His children, is a good business. It is the most constructive, the most permanent, the most satisfying of any enterprise in the world. We should have much satisfaction in the fact that we are part of that business, and that we have some of the responsibility of being a good businessman in that business.

24

They Died For Us

In August, 1975, my wife and I had the privilege of spending time in the Philippine Islands. One of the highlights of this experience was our visit to beautiful Fort Bonafacio Cemetery. This cemetery was formerly known as Fort McKinley, so named in honor of President McKinley. But because of the international nature of the cemetery, the name was changed to the one presently in use.

This cemetery has been beautifully landscaped, and a memorial has been built to those who gave their lives to repel the onslaught of Japanese agressors who had in their hearts infamous ideas of conquest. The chief part of the landscaping is made up of seventeen thousand white crosses, each one marking the resting place of an American soldier who gave his life for his country and its citizens who stayed at home. In an inscription in the cemetery are four simple words which recount the virtues of these heroes by saying, "They died for us."

All my life I have been impressed with sacrifices that have been made by other people with me as the beneficiary. I have tried to appreciate my benefactors as much as possible but it is often easy for us, as beneficiaries, to proceed as usual without showing proper appreciation, while our benefactors are making noteworthy sacrifices in our interest.

These young men who died in World War II left their homes, their studies, their friends, and their sweethearts to serve their country. Their lives were cut off almost before they began.

These young men loved life. They were full of ambition. They had high expectations. They wanted to marry eventually and have a family and an occupation of their own. They wanted to have the thrill of accomplishment in the various fields that life would offer them. They wanted to have grandchildren, to grow old, and to finish their life's probation in the ordinary and ordained way.

But they didn't. They died in a foreign land, thousands of miles from home, in the prime of their youth. They were denied the comforting ministrations of loved ones while they themselves were engaged in the herculean task of trying to stop the cruel aggression of a brutal, merciless Japanese army. As I stood amid the crosses on that beautiful summer day, I tried to build a still greater appreciation for these young soldiers, both American and Philippino, who had given freely of the most precious possession in the world—life itself—for my benefit, peace, and comfort. Engraved in my heart was this memory: "They died for us."

After returning home, I tried to go deeper into this situation in my contemplation. We were just beginning our bicentennial year in America, and I thought of Revolutionary soldiers who also gave their lives that we might be free to enjoy the blessings to which this nation, under God, was entitled. These soldiers died so that a new nation might live and enjoy a new birth of freedom.

I meditated about those courageous and inspired men who became our founding Fathers; men who stood in the forefront of our civilization to give our nation its start toward its destiny. On that important day of July 4, 1776, they signed the great Declaration of Independence in which they said that America was, and ought to be, a free and independent nation. Then, above their signatures, they wrote:

"And for the support of this declaration, with a firm reliance on the protection of Divine Providence, we mutually pledge to each other our lives, our fortunes, and our sacred honor."

A book has been written about this event in world history under the title "They Signed For Us." When they made this historic compact representing our interests, they were fully aware that if their enterprise should fail, their heads would fall; even as it was, many of them gave their lives and their fortunes. Our founding fathers not only signed the Declaration for us, but a large number of them literally died for us.

Fifty-six men signed the Declaration of Independence. They pledged their lives, and at least nine of them died as a result of the war. If the Revolution had failed, if their fight had come to naught, the rest would have been hanged as traitors. They pledged their fortunes, and at least fifteen fulfilled that pledge in supporting the war effort. They pledged their sacred honor.

This devotion was best expressed by the noble statement of John Adams. He said, "All that I have, and all that I am, and all that I hope, in this life, I am now ready here to stake upon it; and I leave off as I began, that live or die, survive or perish, I am for the Declaration of Independence. It is my living sentiment, and by the blessing of God, it shall be my dying sentiment, Independence now, and INDEPENDENCE FOREVER." (*Works of Daniel Webster,* Boston: Little, Brown & Co., 1877, 17th Ed., 1:135.) How fitting it is that we sing:

O beautiful for heroes proved
In liberating strife,
Who more than self their country loved,
And mercy more than life!

It may be startling to some that we have heard from the signers of the Declaration since they departed from this life. During the period when Wilford Woodruff was president of the St. George Temple, the Founding Fathers, with George Washington at their head, appeared to him and requested that their temple work be done. President Woodruff testified that these founders of our republic pointed out to him that they had laid the foundation of the government we now enjoy, they had remained true to it and that they had also remained faithful to God (see Journal of Discourses, 19:229).

President Woodruff said that those men who laid the foundation of this American government and who signed the Declaration of Independence were the best men the God of heaven could find on the face of the earth. They were noble spirits. General Washington and all those who labored for the establishment of our government were inspired of the Lord. (See *Conference Report,* April 1898, p. 89.)

We should thank God for the sacrifices and efforts made by these Founding Fathers, whose efforts have brought us both the blessings of political liberty and the economic prosperity we enjoy today. Their lives should be reminders to us that we are the blessed beneficiaries of a liberty earned by sacrifices of property, reputation, and life.

In the final analysis, what the framers of the Constitution did, under the inspiration of God, was to draft a document that merited the approval of God himself, who declared that it should "be maintained for the rights and protection of *all* flesh" (D&C101:77).

The Constitution has been criticized by some as outmoded, and even a recent president of the United States criticized it as a document "written for an entirely different period in our nation's history" (*U. S. News and World Report,* Dec. 17, 1962, p. 104). The eminent constitutional authority, President J. Reuben Clark, Jr., answered the argument in these words:

"There were the horse and buggy days as they have been called in derision; these were the men who traveled in the horse-drawn buggies and on horseback; but these were the men who carried under their hats, as they rode in the buggies and on their horses, a political wisdom garnered from the ages" (Clark, *Stand Fast by Our Constitution,* p. 136).

What those framers did can be better appreciated when it is considered that when the instrument went into operation, it covered only thirteen states with a population of fewer than four million people. Today our constitution adequately covers fifty states with over two hundred million people.

The wisdom of these delegates is shown in the genius of the document itself. Since the founders had a strong distrust for centralized power in a federal government, they created a government with checks and balances to prevent any branch of government from becoming too powerful.

Congress could pass laws, but the president could check this with a veto. Congress, however, could override the veto, and by its means of initiative in taxation, could further restrain the executive department. The Supreme Court could nullify laws made by the Congress.

God redeemed the land by the shedding of blood. This land has been fertilized by the blood of patriots. During the struggle for independence, nearly nine thousand colonists were killed.

At the close of the Revolution, the thirteen states found themselves independent but faced with grave internal economic and political problems. The Articles of Confederation had been adopted but proved to be ineffectual. Under this instrument, the nation was without a president, a head. There was a congress, but it was a body destitute of any power. There was no Supreme Court. The states were merely a confederation.

Washington wrote of the defects of this loose federation in these words: "The fabrick which took nine years, at the expense of much blood and treasure to rear, now totters to the foundation, and without support must soon fall" (John C. Fitzpatrick, ed., *Writing of George Washington,* Washington, D.C.: Government Printing Office, 1939, 29:68). Because of this crisis, fifty-five of the seventy-four appointed delegates reported to the convention, representing every state except Rhode Island, for the purpose of forming "a more perfect union." Thirty-nine finally signed the Constitution.

Who were these delegates, those whom the Lord designated "wise men" whom He raised up? They were mostly young men in the prime of life, their average age being forty-four. Benjamin Franklin was the eldest at eighty-one. George Washington, the presiding officer at the convention, was fifty-five. Alexander Hamilton was only thirty-two; James Madison, who recorded the proceedings of the convention with his remarkable *Notes,* was only thirty-six. These were young men, but men of exceptional character, "sober, seasoned, distinguished men of affairs, drawn from various walks of life" (J. Reuben Clark, Jr., *Stand Fast by Our Constitution,* Deseret Book Co., 1965, p. 135).

As I stood among the dead at the cemetery in the Philippines, I thought of other cemeteries around the world where other crosses represent the burial place of other soldiers who gave their lives for us. There is a cemetery at Pearl Harbor where a sneak attack by the Japanese destroyed the lives of many people. I thought of those life-giving statements of Jesus who said, "It is more blessed to give than to receive."

We have at present a group of Americans who think of themselves as the downtrodden, the persecuted. They want to point out injustices done to them. What most concerns them is how to get, rather than how to serve. Jesus may have intended another statement primarily for them when He said, "He that looseth his life for my sake shall find it."

To sacrifice ourselves for the welfare of others is far more profitable than is egotistical self-seeking. This is indicated in other cemeteries where it is evident that other people gave their lives, not only to win our independence, but to maintain our various freedoms, our standards of living, and our way of life.

We have cemeteries of the Civil War, which was not caused by the invasion of a foreign foe, but by a fraternal strife which threatened to divide and to destroy our country from within. This war proved to be the most costly war that was ever fought so far as American lives and property are concerned.

But other people have given their lives for us who did not take up arms against a personal foe. We have suffered more defeats and lost more values during years of peace than during years of war. Many others have given their lives to protect us from traitors from within, from criminals, from disloyal, ungodly Americans who have tried to sabotage our country, destroy our faith, and subjugate our land by supporting idlers, un-American ne'er-do-wells and those who would cheat and weaken the country and bleed it of material, intellectual and moral resources.

A battlefield is not the only place where heroes, patriots, leaders, and ordinary, true-blue Americans give up their lives for others. In the vast amount of aid furnished to the peoples of the world by Americans, everyone has literally given a part of his life's energy that people less fortunate than we might have life and have it more abundantly.

Others have given their lives to scientific research or to fields of human service and betterment. Others have fought to maintain the strengths and faith so necessary to our greatest human success.

> So he died for his faith, that was fine—
> More than most of us do.
> But say, can you add to that line
> That he lived for it too?

As we think of what other people have done for us and of the deaths they have died, we might think of the sepulcher at Golgotha, and the sacrifice that even the Son of God made for us, or we might think of the lines of Julia Ward Howe:

> In the beauty of the lilies,
> Christ was born across the sea
> With a glory in his bosom

That transfigures you and me.
As he died to make men holy
Let us die to make them free,
For God is marching on.

Marie Sklodowska, a Polish girl who married the French physicist, Pierre Curie, devoted much of her life to research. They worked for many years together without funds and without aid, as they tried to isolate radium from a low-grade uranium ore called "pitchblende." After their 487th experiment had failed, Pierre threw up his hands in despair and said, "It will never be done. Maybe in a hundred years, but never in our day." Marie confronted him with a resolute face and said, "If it takes a hundred years it will be a pity, but I will not cease to work for it was long as I live."

Finally, when their labors met with success, they were in a position to make millions of dollars by patenting their famous discovery; but the Curies refused to take a patent. Their discovery was something they felt belonged to all the world, and they would not allow themselves to make a profit by it.

In 1934, Madam Curie died at age sixty-seven from radium burns received from her discovery. On Friday, July 6, 1934, at noon, without speeches or processions, without a politician or an official present, Madam Curie took a modest place in the realm of the dead. She was buried beside Pierre in the cemetery at Sceaux, in the presence of her relatives, her friends and the co-workers who loved her. So we might also place over her grave a statement saying, "She died for us."

George Bernard Shaw sums up this philosophy of service to others. He said, "I am of the opinion that my life belongs to the whole community and as long as I live, it is my privilege to do for it whatsoever I can. I want to be thoroughly used up when I die, for the harder I work the more I live. I enjoy life for its own sake. Life is no brief candle for me; it is a splendid torch which I may hold for a moment and I want to make it burn as brightly as possible before handing it on to future generations. The test of true character is the ability to carry out a worthy resolution long after the mood in which it was made has changed."

I myself happen to be one of a family of ten children. When this family was formed, my mother and father were young and vigorous and in the best of health. They had been given an allotment of time from life; and as the children were born, our parents began to use their supply of energy in our behalf. Fortunately for us, the supply lasted until most of us were grown and self-supporting; and when the supply was gone, my father and mother died. And so our family might say of our parents, "They died for us."

Some one hundred and fifty years ago, someone, seeking to lessen the financial effects of death, invented the idea of life insurance. Through life insurance one may add another benefit to be paid to his family in cash when he dies. In the enormous insurance industries throughout the world, hundreds of thousands of people will die every year; and as a result of their foresightedness mortgages will be paid, widows will be given incomes and orphans will be sent to school. In this way, in addition to dying for their children, parents may postpone the financial effects of their deaths until their children are properly educated. Thus millions of dependent children every year can say of their deceased, but insured, parents, "They died for us."

Therefore we may erect monuments in the memory of our many "parental" soldiers both known and unknown and say, "They died for us."

At Guadalcanal, a beautiful monument has been erected where an entire Marine regiment was wiped out during World War II. Not one Marine survived. On this monument is an inscription which reads, "When you go home, tell them of us and say, for their tomorrows we gave our todays."

We who survive may take up the cry of the Marines on Guadalcanal and give our todays that others may have beautiful and happy tomorrows.

25

The Three Degrees Of Glory

Certainly one of the best resources we have as human beings to make our lives successful is the word of the Lord. The scriptures indicate that no man by searching can find God (Job 11:7). We are dependent for our knowledge of God on those revelations which He has given to us by direct contact through His prophets. And through this process, the Lord promised us many wonderful blessings.

As He approached the end of His mortal life, the Lord said to His followers:

"In my Father's house are many mansions: if it were not so, I would have told you. I go to prepare a place for you.

"And if I go and prepare a place for you, I will come again, and receive you unto myself; that where I am, there ye may be also." (John 14:2-3.)

It is a challenging thought to try to understand the glory that would be evidenced by mansions in heaven created by the great God of heaven and earth. About the magnificence of God's gift to us, Paul has said:

". . . Eye hath not seen, nor ear heard, neither have entered into the heart of man, the things which God hath prepared for them that love him" (1 Cor. 2:9).

In further explanation of this mansion-in-heaven program, the Apostle Paul said to the Corinthians:

"There are also celestial bodies, and bodies terrestrial: but the glory of the celestial is one, and the glory of the terrestrial is another.

"There is one glory of the sun, and another glory of the moon, and another glory of the stars: for one star differeth from another star in glory.

"So also is the resurrection of the dead." (1 Cor. 15:40-43.)

In our own day the Lord has given a revelation describing in detail these three glories and who will inhabit them. This revelation is contained in the 76th section of the Doctrine and Covenants.

In writing a preview for this revelation, the Prophet Joseph Smith made the following explanation:

"Upon my return from Amherst conference, I resumed the translation of the Scriptures. From sundry revelations which had been received, it was apparent that many important points touching the salvation of man had been taken from the Bible, or lost before it was compiled. It appeared self-evident from what truths were left, that if God rewarded every one according to the deeds done in the body, the term 'Heaven,' as intended for the Saints' eternal home, must include more kingdoms than one."

And while Joseph Smith and Sidney Rigdon were engaged in prayerful consideration of this matter, it was made known to them in this revelation that there are three primary degrees of glory.

Other scriptures indicate that there is more than one kingdom. Paul tells of a man in his day who was caught up into the third heaven (2 Cor. 12:2). In Deuteronomy 10:14, Moses mentions the heaven of heavens. And in the 131st section of the Doctrine & Covenants, we are told that even in the celestial kingdom there are three separate degrees of glory.

The three degrees of glory indicated by Paul were the celestial, which could be likened to the glory of the noon-day sun; the terrestrial, which Paul likened to the lesser light of the moon; and the telestial, which by comparison could best be described by the twinkle of the stars.

It is important that we give this revelation much study. And to make it easier, I am placing all of the verses pertaining to each kingdom together. It might be advisable for anyone interested in making an intensive study of this revelation to read the entire section first and then give special attention to each individual section by reading the specific verses which apply to that kingdom or glory.

The Celestial Kingdom

The verses contained in the 76th section of the Doctrine and Covenants pertaining to the celestial kingdom are as follows:

50. And again we bear record—for we saw and heard, and this is the testimony of the gospel of Christ concerning them who shall come forth in the resurrection of the just—

51. They are they who received the testimony of Jesus, and believed on his name and were baptized after the manner of his burial, being buried in the water in his name, and this according to the commandment which he has given—

52. That by keeping the commandments they might be washed and cleansed from all their sins, and receive the Holy Spirit by the laying on of hands of him who is ordained and sealed unto this power.

53. And who overcome by faith, and are sealed by the Holy Spirit of promise, which the Father sheds forth upon all those who are just and true.

54. They are they who are the church of the Firstborn.

55. They are they into whose hands the Father has given all things—

56. They are they who are priests and kings, who have received of his fulness, and of his glory;

57. And are priests of the Most High, after the order of Melchizedek, which was after the order of Enoch, which was after the order of the Only Begotten Son.

58. Wherefore, as it is written, they are gods, even the sons of God—

59. Wherefore, all things are theirs, whether life or death, or things present, or things to come, all are theirs and they are Christ's, and Christ is God's.

60. And they shall overcome all things.

61. Wherefore, let no man glory in man, but rather let him glory in God, who shall subdue all enemies under his feet.

62. These shall dwell in the presence of God and his Christ forever and ever.

63. These are they whom he shall bring with him, when he shall come in the clouds of heaven to reign on the earth over his people.

64. These are they who shall have part in the first resurrection.

65. These are they who shall come forth in the resurrection of the just.

66. These are they who are come unto Mount Zion, and unto the city of the living God, the heavenly place, the holiest of all.

67. These are they who have come to an innumerable company of angels, to the general assembly and church of Enoch, and of the Firstborn.

68. These are they whose names are written in heaven, where God and Christ are the judge of all.

69. These are they who are just men made perfect through Jesus the mediator of the new covenant, who wrought out this perfect atonement through the shedding of his own blood.

70. These are they whose bodies are celestial, whose glory is that of the sun, even the glory of God, the highest of all, whose glory the sun of the firmament is written of as being typical . . .

92. And thus we saw the glory of the celestial, which excels in all things—where God, even the Father, reigns upon his throne forever and ever;

93. Before whose throne all things bow in humble reverence, and give him glory forever and ever.

94. They who dwell in his presence are the church of the First-born; and they see as they are seen, and know as they are known, having received of his fulness and of his grace;

95. And he makes them equal in power, and in might, and in dominion.

96. And the glory of the celestial is one, even as the glory of the sun is one.

Section 88, verses 18 through 20 say more about the celestial kingdom:

18. Therefore, (the earth) must needs be sanctified from all unrighteousness, that it may be prepared for the celestial glory;

19. For after it hath filled the measure of its creation, it shall be crowned with glory, even with the presence of God the Father;

20. That bodies who are of the celestial kingdom may possess it forever and ever; for, for this intent was it made and created, and for this intent are they sanctified.

Some of the conditions of the celestial kingdom are described in the 131st section of the Doctrine and Covenants, verses 1 through 4:

1. In the celestial glory there are three heavens or degrees;

2. And in order to obtain the highest, a man must enter into this order of the priesthood (meaning the new and everlasting covenant of marriage);

3. And if he does not, he cannot obtain it.

4. He may enter into the other, but that is the end of his kingdom; he cannot have an increase.

The Terrestrial Kingdom

The following is from the 76th section of the Doctrine and Covenants, verses 71 through 80:

71. And again, we saw the terrestrial world, and behold and lo, these are they who are of the terrestrial, whose glory differs from that of the church of the Firstborn who have received the fulness of the Father, even as that of the moon differs from the sun in the firmament.

72. Behold, these are they who died without law;

73. And also they who are the spirits of men kept in prison, whom the Son visited, and preached the gospel unto them, that they might be judged according to men in the flesh.

74. Who received not the testimony of Jesus in the flesh, but afterwards received it.

75. These are they who are honorable men of the earth, who were blinded by the craftiness of men.

76. These are they who receive of his glory, but not of his fulness.

77. These are they who receive of the presence of the Son, but not of the fulness of the Father.

78. Wherefore, they are bodies terrestrial, and not bodies celestial, and differ in glory as the moon differs from the sun.

79. These are they who are not valiant in the testimony of Jesus; wherefore, they obtain not the crown over the kingdom of our God.

80. And now this is the end of the vision which we saw of the terrestrial, that the Lord commanded us to write while we were yet in the Spirit.

91. And thus we saw the glory of the terrestrial which excels in all things the glory of the telestial, even in glory, and in power, and in might, and in dominion.

97. And the glory of the terrestrial is one, even as the glory of the moon is one.

The following information in section 88, verse 23, also appears specifically to be related to the terrestrial kingdom:

23. And he who cannot abide the law
    of a terrestrial kingdom cannot
    abide a terrestrial glory.

The Telestial Kingdom

The following verses in section 76 of the Doctrine and Covenants refer specifically to the telestial kingdom:

81. And again, we saw the glory of the telestial, which glory is that of the lesser, even as the glory of the stars differs from that of the glory of the moon in the firmament.

82. These are they who received not the gospel of Christ, neither the testimony of Jesus.

83. These are they who deny not the Holy Spirit.

84. These are they who are thrust down to hell.

85. These are they who shall not be redeemed from the devil until the last resurrection, until the Lord even Christ the Lamb, shall have finished his work.

86. These are they who receive not of his fulness in the eternal world, but of the Holy Spirit through the ministration of the terrestrial;

87. And the terrestrial through the ministration of the celestial.

88. And also the telestial receive it of the administering of angels who are appointed to minister for them, or who are appointed to be ministering spirits for them; for they shall be heirs of salvation.

89. And thus we saw, in the heavenly vision, the glory of the telestial, which surpasses all understanding;

98. And the glory of the telestial is one, even as the glory of the stars is one;

for as one star differs from another star in glory, even so differs one from another in glory in the telestial world;

99. For these are they who are of Paul, and of Appollos, and of Cephas.

100. These are they who say they are some of one and some of another— some of Christ and some of John, and some of Moses, and some of Elias, and some of Esaias, and some of Isaiah, and some of Enoch;

101. But received not the gospel, neither the testimony of Jesus, neither the prophets, neither the everlasting covenant.

102. Last of all, these all are they who will not be gathered with the saints, to be caught up unto the church of the Firstborn, and received into the cloud.

103. These are they who are liars, and sorcerers, and adulterers, and whoremongers, and whosoever loves and makes a lie.

104. These are they who suffer the wrath of God on earth.

105. These are they who suffer the vengeance of eternal fire.

106. These are they who are cast down to hell and suffer the wrath of Almighty God, until the fulness of times, when Christ shall have subdued all enemies under his feet, and shall have perfected his work;

107. When he shall deliver up the kingdom, and present it unto the Father, spotless, saying: I have overcome and have trodden the wine-press alone, even the wine-press of the fierceness of the wrath of Almighty God.

108. Then shall he be crowned with the crown of his glory, to sit on the throne of his power to reign forever and ever.

109. But behold, and lo, we saw the glory and the inhabitants of the telestial world, that they were as innumerable as the stars in the firmament of heaven, or as the sand upon the seashore;

110. And heard the voice of the Lord saying: These all shall bow the knee, and every tongue shall confess to him who sits upon the throne forever and ever;

111. For they shall be judged according to their works, and every man shall receive according to his own works, his own dominion, in the mansions which are prepared;

112. And they shall be servants of the Most High; but where God and Christ dwell they cannot come, worlds without end.

The following verse from section 88 also refers to the telestial kingdom:

24. And he who cannot abide the law of a telestial kingdom cannot abide a telestial glory; therefore he is not meet for a kingdom of glory. Therefore he must abide a kingdom which is not a kingdom of glory.

Sons of Perdition

There is also a kingdom in eternity which is not a kingdom of glory. This is inhabited by the sons of perdition who followed the rebellion of Lucifer in the Council in Heaven. Those who belong to this kingdom are the only ones who will not be redeemed in the due time of the Lord.

Doctrine and Covenants, section 76, verses 25 through 49, say:

25. And this we saw also, and bear record, that an angel of God who was in authority in the presence of God, who rebelled against the Only Begotten Son whom the Father loved and who was in the bosom of the Father, was thrust down from the presence of God and the Son,

26. And was called Perdition, for the heavens wept over him—he was Lucifer, a son of the morning.

27. And we beheld, and lo, he is fallen! is fallen, even a son of the morning!

28. And while we were yet in the Spirit, the Lord commanded us that we should write the vision; for we beheld Satan, that old serpent, even the devil, who rebelled against God, and sought to take the kingdom of our God and his Christ—

29. Wherefore, he maketh war with the saints of God, and encompasseth them round about.

30. And we saw a vision of the sufferings of those with whom he made war and overcame, for thus came the voice of the Lord unto us:

31. Thus saith the Lord concerning all those who know my power, and have been partakers thereof, and suffered themselves through the power of the devil to be overcome, and to deny the truth and defy my power—

32. They are they who are the sons of perdition, of whom I say that it had been better for them never to have been born;

33. For they are vessels of wrath, doomed to suffer the wrath of God, with the devil and his angels in eternity;

34. Concerning whom I have said there is no forgiveness in this world nor in the world to come—

35. Having denied the Holy Spirit after having received it, and having denied the Only Begotten Son of the Father, having crucified him unto themselves and put him to an open shame.

36. These are they who shall go away into the lake of fire and brimstone, with the devil and his angels—

37. The only ones on whom the second death shall have any power;

38. Yea, verily, the only ones who shall not be redeemed in the due time of the Lord, after the sufferings of his wrath.

39. For all the rest shall be brought forth by the resurrection of the dead, through the triumph and the glory of the Lamb, who was slain, who was in the bosom of the Father before the worlds were made.

40. And this is the gospel, the glad tidings, which the voice out of the heavens bore record unto us—

41. That he came into the world, even Jesus, to be crucified for the world, and to bear the sins of the world,

and to sanctify the world, and to cleanse it from all unrighteousness;

42. That through him all might be saved whom the Father had put into his power and made by him;

43. Who glorifies the Father, and saves all the works of his hands, except those sons of perdition who deny the Son after the Father has him.

44. Wherefore, he saves all except them—they shall go away into everlasting punishment, which is endless punishment, which is eternal punishment, to reign with the devil and his angels in eternity, where their worm dieth not, and the fire is not quenched, which is their torment—

45. And the end thereof, neither the place thereof, nor their torment, no man knows;

46. Neither was it revealed, neither is neither will be revealed unto man, except to them who are made partakers thereof;

47. Nevertheless, I, the Lord, show it by vision unto many, but straightway shut it up again;

48. Wherefore, the end, the width, the height, the depth, and the misery thereof, they understand not, neither any man except those who are ordained unto this condemnation.

49. And we heard the voice, saying: Write the vision of the sufferings of the ungodly.

Paul describes to the Hebrews the magnitude of becoming a son of perdition as follows:

4. For it is impossible for those who were once enlightened, and have tasted of the heavenly gift, and were made partakers of the Holy Ghost,

5. And have tasted the good word of God, and the powers of the world to come,

6. If they shall fall away, to renew them again unto repentance; seeing they crucify to themselves the Son of God afresh, and put him to an open shame. (Hebrews 6:4-6.)